Unity 2017 Game AI Programming
Third Edition

Leverage the power of Artificial Intelligence to program smart entities for your games

Ray Barrera
Aung Sithu Kyaw
Thet Naing Swe

BIRMINGHAM - MUMBAI

Unity 2017 Game AI Programming
Third Edition

Commissioning Editor: Kunal Chaudhari
Acquisition Editor: Reshma Raman
Content Development Editor: Francis Carneiro
Technical Editor: Murtaza Tinwala
Copy Editor: Safis Editing
Project Coordinator: Devanshi Doshi
Proofreader: Safis Editing
Indexer: Tejal Daruwale Soni
Graphics: Jason Monteiro
Production Coordinator: Shraddha Falebhai

First published: July 2013
Second edition: September 2015
Third edition: January 2018

Production reference: 2050318

Published by Packt Publishing Ltd.
Livery Place
35 Livery Street
Birmingham
B3 2PB, UK.

ISBN 978-1-78847-790-1

www.packtpub.com

`mapt.io`

Mapt is an online digital library that gives you full access to over 5,000 books and videos, as well as industry leading tools to help you plan your personal development and advance your career. For more information, please visit our website.

Why subscribe?

- Spend less time learning and more time coding with practical eBooks and Videos from over 4,000 industry professionals

- Improve your learning with Skill Plans built especially for you

- Get a free eBook or video every month

- Mapt is fully searchable

- Copy and paste, print, and bookmark content

PacktPub.com

Did you know that Packt offers eBook versions of every book published, with PDF and ePub files available? You can upgrade to the eBook version at `www.PacktPub.com` and as a print book customer, you are entitled to a discount on the eBook copy. Get in touch with us at `service@packtpub.com` for more details.

At `www.PacktPub.com`, you can also read a collection of free technical articles, sign up for a range of free newsletters, and receive exclusive discounts and offers on Packt books and eBooks.

Contributors

About the authors

Ray Barrera is a software engineer, who has spent the better part of the decade working on various serious, entertainment and educational projects in Unity. He has spoken at college campuses, and presented a talk at Unite 2017 in Austin, on app development in Unity. He is currently working in education tech as director of mobile engineering at a well-known education company. Free time outside of work is spent on a number of hobbies, including hiking, music, and cooking (primarily Mexican food).

> *I'd like to thank my friends and family and my wonderful fiancee, Cara, who is the most supportive and amazing partner a man could wish for. I would also like to dedicate this book to my amazing mother, Maria, whom I lost earlier this year. She shaped me into the man I am today, and I could not be more thankful to her. I love you and miss you, mom.*

Aung Sithu Kyaw is passionate about graphics programming, creating video games, writing, and sharing knowledge with others. He holds an MSc in digital media technology from the Nanyang Technological University (NTU), Singapore. Lastly, he worked as a research associate, which involved implementing a sensor-based real-time movie system using Unreal Development Kit. In 2011, he founded a tech start-up focusing on interactive media productions and backend server-side technologies.

Thet Naing Swe has been working in the software and game industry for more than 10 years and has a passion for creating all types of games including serious, casual, casino and AAA games.

He received the 1st class Honor Degree in Computer Games Development from University of Central Lancashire, UK in 2008 and started working as a game programmer at CodeMonkey studio for a year before joining NTU Singapore as a graphic programmer using UDK. He founded JoyDash Pte Ltd Singapore in 2014 where it produces casino, casual and multiplayer mobile games mainly for Myanmar market.

About the reviewer

Davide Aversa completed his Master in Robotics and Artificial Intelligence and Ph.D. in Computer Science at La Sapienza University of Rome where he has been involved in research applied to pathfinding and decision making for digital games characters, and computational creativity.

Packt is searching for authors like you

If you're interested in becoming an author for Packt, please visit authors.packtpub.com and apply today. We have worked with thousands of developers and tech professionals, just like you, to help them share their insight with the global tech community. You can make a general application, apply for a specific hot topic that we are recruiting an author for, or submit your own idea.

Table of Contents

Preface

Welcome to the wonderful world of AI in games, or, more specifically, AI in Unity. This book focuses on the Unity implementations of AI-related features and also delves into the basic concepts behind those features. It even provides ground-up examples of some of them. Along the way, this book provides example projects and sample code for the reader to follow, play with, and, hopefully, build upon in their own projects.

Who this book is for

While the reader is not expected to be an advanced programmer, this book does assume some base-level knowledge of C# and scripting in Unity. That said, the sample code provided is well commented and explained throughout the book in a very detailed way, in order to describe the reason behind each decision and every line of code. Familiarity with some of the algorithms provided is certainly helpful, but by no means required. This book will explain the theory and origin of the concepts and then delve into implementations that highlight the core functionality we're looking for. Extraneous code is kept to a minimum to allow the reader to truly focus on the book's main objective—learning AI game programming in Unity.

What this book covers

Chapter 1, *The Basics of AI in Games*, gets the reader up to speed with the basic terminology we'll be working with. In order to build up to the more advanced concepts in the book, we first lay the groundwork and expectations for the following chapters. This introductory chapter provides a preview of some of the concepts covered and prepares the reader with the necessary knowledge to be successful in the sample projects and code to follow.

Chapter 2, *Finite State Machines and You*, jumps right into one of the most essential concepts in game AI--the finite state machine. The chapter starts with a conceptual overview and then dives into an implementation of a state machine in Unity using the built-in features, such as Mecanim and StateMachineBehaviours. This chapter is the first to take the user through an actual example and sets the tone for how future chapters will explain the concepts they cover.

Chapter 3, *Implementing Sensors*, builds on the concept of the AI agent by providing the reader the knowledge and techniques to make their AI more believable. In this chapter, the reader learns how to implement sensing for their agents, allowing them to collect data and information from their virtual surroundings, thus enabling more complex interactions with their environment. The output of the agent is only as good as the input, and this chapter ensures that the reader can implement sensing mechanisms to give AI behaviors solid inputs to base their algorithms on.

Chapter 4, *Finding Your Way*, takes the reader's knowledge to the next level. With the skills from the previous three chapters to build on, the reader is now given the tools to have their AI agent navigate the game world. A few different alternatives are explained in detail, such as node-based pathfinding, the near-standard A* algorithm approach, and finally, Unity's NavMesh system. Examples are provided for each, and the user is given the necessary knowledge to pick the right approach for each situation.

Chapter 5, *Flocks and Crowds*, covers the history and implementation of a standard flocking algorithm. Along with some history on the topic, the user is walked through a sample project that implements flocking to create convincing boid systems to model birds, fish, locusts, or any other flocking behavior. In the later portion of the chapter, the reader is introduced to implementing simple crowd dynamics using Unity's NavMesh system. Once again, sample scenes are provided to illustrate the different implementations.

Chapter 6, *Behavior Trees*, showcases another handy tool in the AI game programmer's tool belt: the behavior tree. The chapter teaches readers the concepts behind behavior trees, walks them through a custom implementation, and applies the knowledge learned in two examples: a simple math-based example and a more fun and frankly silly example we call HomeRock, which emulates a popular online card game to showcase behavior trees in action.

Chapter 7, *Using Fuzzy Logic to Make Your AI Seem Alive*, sets the stage with a long and descriptive title, right? This chapter covers the fundamental concepts in fuzzy logic and the approach for converting fuzzy values to concrete values and explains a simple approach for implementing fuzzy logic in Unity. The first example illustrates the simplest possible version of the concepts, and the second example illustrates a morality/faction system like you'd find in an RPG to illustrate the usefulness of fuzzy logic.

Chapter 8, *How It All Comes Together*, takes concepts the reader has learned throughout the book and throws them into a sample tower defense example project. This chapter illustrates how, by taking a handful of AI techniques, you can quickly throw together a game that implements AI NPCs and enemies and gives them rudimentary decision-making abilities.

To get the most out of this book

1. Be sure to download all the sample code for this book! Following along with the examples is crucial to understanding all the concepts covered.
2. Brush up on your C# if you're rusty. This book will do its best to not leave anyone behind, but a beginner to intermediate level of understanding of C# and Unity scripting is assumed.
3. Experiment! This book covers the core concepts, but all the examples are set up for experimentation. The reader is encouraged to build upon the given examples, to tweak values, assets, and code to achieve new outcomes.
4. Be patient. Depending on your skill level or experience, you may find some of these concepts a bit daunting. Be sure to follow the instructions closely, and examine all the provided sample code thoroughly. AI can be a daunting subject, and while this book aims to make you feel comfortable with the core concepts, it's OK if you need to read an example more than once to fully understand all the nuances.

Download the example code files

You can download the example code files for this book from your account at `www.packtpub.com`. If you purchased this book elsewhere, you can visit `www.packtpub.com/support` and register to have the files emailed directly to you.

You can download the code files by following these steps:

1. Log in or register at `www.packtpub.com`.
2. Select the **SUPPORT** tab.
3. Click on **Code Downloads & Errata**.
4. Enter the name of the book in the **Search** box and follow the onscreen instructions.

Once the file is downloaded, please make sure that you unzip or extract the folder using the latest version of:

- WinRAR/7-Zip for Windows
- Zipeg/iZip/UnRarX for Mac
- 7-Zip/PeaZip for Linux

The code bundle for the book is also hosted on GitHub at `https://github.com/PacktPublishing/Unity-2017-Game-AI-Programming-Third-Edition`. We also have other code bundles from our rich catalog of books and videos available at `https://github.com/PacktPublishing/`. Check them out!

Download the color images

We also provide a PDF file that has color images of the screenshots/diagrams used in this book. You can download it here: `http://www.packtpub.com/sites/default/files/downloads/Unity2017GameAIProgrammingThirdEdition_ColorImages.pdf`.

Code in Action

Visit the following link to check out videos of the code being run:
`https://goo.gl/rWXbwZ`

Conventions used

There are a number of text conventions used throughout this book.

`CodeInText`: Indicates code words in text, database table names, folder names, filenames, file extensions, pathnames, dummy URLs, user input, and Twitter handles. Here is an example: "In fact, behaviors derive from `ScriptableObject`, not `MonoBehaviour`, so they exist only as assets."

A block of code is set as follows:

```
private int currentTarget;
private float distanceFromTarget;
private Transform[] waypoints = null;
```

Bold: Indicates a new term, an important word, or words that you see onscreen. For example, words in menus or dialog boxes appear in the text like this. Here is an example: "As you can see in the previous screenshot, we have **Show Grid** set to true."

 Warnings or important notes appear like this.

Tips and tricks appear like this.

Get in touch

Feedback from our readers is always welcome.

General feedback: Email `feedback@packtpub.com` and mention the book title in the subject of your message. If you have questions about any aspect of this book, please email us at `questions@packtpub.com`.

Errata: Although we have taken every care to ensure the accuracy of our content, mistakes do happen. If you have found a mistake in this book, we would be grateful if you would report this to us. Please visit `www.packtpub.com/submit-errata`, selecting your book, clicking on the Errata Submission Form link, and entering the details.

Piracy: If you come across any illegal copies of our works in any form on the Internet, we would be grateful if you would provide us with the location address or website name. Please contact us at `copyright@packtpub.com` with a link to the material.

If you are interested in becoming an author: If there is a topic that you have expertise in and you are interested in either writing or contributing to a book, please visit `authors.packtpub.com`.

Reviews

Please leave a review. Once you have read and used this book, why not leave a review on the site that you purchased it from? Potential readers can then see and use your unbiased opinion to make purchase decisions, we at Packt can understand what you think about our products, and our authors can see your feedback on their book. Thank you!

For more information about Packt, please visit `packtpub.com`.

1
The Basics of AI in Games

Artificial Intelligence (**AI**) is a rich and complex topic. At first glance, it can seem intimidating. The uses for it are diverse, ranging from robotics to statistics and to (more relevantly for us) entertainment, more specifically, video games. Our goal in this book will be to demystify the subject by breaking down the usage of AI into relatable, applicable solutions, and to provide accessible examples that illustrate the concepts in ways that cut through the noise and go straight for the core ideas. This book will lead you head first into the world of AI, and will introduce you to the most important concepts to start you on your AI journey.

This chapter will give you a little background on AI in academics, traditional domains, and game-specific applications. Here are the topics we'll cover:

- Exploring how the application and implementation of AI in games is different from other domains
- Looking at the special requirements for AI in games
- Looking at the basic AI patterns used in games

This chapter will serve as a reference for later chapters, where we'll implement AI patterns in Unity.

Creating the illusion of life

Before diving in much deeper, we should stop for a moment and define intelligence. Intelligence is simply the ability to learn something then apply that knowledge. Artificial intelligence, at least for our purposes, is the illusion of intelligence. Our intelligent entities need not necessarily learn things, but must at the very least convince the player that they are learning things. I must stress that these definitions fit game AI specifically. As we'll discover later in this section, there are many applications for AI outside of games, where other definitions are more adequate.

Intelligent creatures, such as humans and other animals, learn from their environment. Whether it's through observing something visually, hearing it, feeling it, and so on, our brains convert those stimuli into information that we process and learn from. Similarly, our computer-created AI must observe and react to its environment to appear smart. While we use our eyes, ears, and other means to perceive, our game's AI entities have a different set of sensors at their disposal. Rather than using big, complex brains like ours, our code will simulate the processing of that data and the behaviors that model a logical and believable reaction to that data.

AI and its many related studies are dense and varied, but it is important to understand the basics of AI being used in different domains before digging deeper into the subject. AI is just a general term; its various implementations and applications are different for different needs and for solving different sets of problems.

Before we move onto game-specific techniques, let's take a look at the following research areas in AI applications that have advanced tremendously over the last several decades. Things that used to be considered science fiction are quickly becoming science fact, such as autonomous robots and self-driving cars. You need not look very far to find great examples of advances in AI—your smartphone most likely has a digital assistant feature that relies on some new AI-related technology. It probably knows your schedule better than you do! Here are some of the research fields driving AI:

- **Computer vision**: This is the ability to take visual input from sources, such as video and photo cameras, and analyze it to perform particular operations such as facial recognition, object recognition, and optical-character recognition. Computer vision is at the forefront of advances in autonomous vehicles. Cars with even relatively simple systems, such as collision mitigation and adaptive cruise control, use an array of sensors to determine depth contextually to help prevent collisions.

- **Natural language processing (NLP)**: This is the ability that allows a machine to read and understand the languages as we normally write and speak. The problem is that the languages we use today are difficult for machines to understand. There are many different ways to say the same thing, and the same sentence can have different meanings according to the context. NLP is an important step for machines since they need to understand the languages and expressions we use before they can process them and respond accordingly. Fortunately, there's an enormous number of datasets available on the web that can help researchers by doing automatic analysis of a language.
- **Common sense reasoning**: This is a technique that our brains can easily use to draw answers even from domains we don't fully understand. Common sense knowledge is a usual and common way for us to attempt certain questions since our brains can mix and interplay context, background knowledge, and language proficiency. But making machines apply such knowledge is very complex and still a major challenge for researchers.
- **Machine learning**: This may sound like something straight out of a science fiction movie, and the reality is not too far off. Computer programs generally consist of a static set of instructions, which take input and provide output. Machine learning focuses on the science of writing algorithms and programs that can learn from the data processed by said program, and apply that for future learning.

Neural Networks

After years and years of research and development, AI is a rapidly expanding field. As consumer-level computer hardware becomes more and more powerful, developers are finding new and exciting ways to implement ever complex forms of AI in all kinds of applications. One such AI concept is **Neural Networks**, a subset of machine learning that we mentioned in the previous section. Neural Networks enable computers to "learn", and through repeated training become more and more efficient and effective at solving any number of problems. A very popular exercise for testing Neural Network machine learning is teaching an AI how to discern the value of a set of handwritten numbers.

In what we call **supervised learning**, we provide our Neural Network a set of training data. In the handwritten number scenario, we pass in hundreds or thousands of images collected from any source containing handwritten numbers. Using a process called **back propagation**, the network can adjust itself with the values and data it just "learned" to create a more accurate prediction in the next iteration of the learning cycle.

Believe it or not, the concept of Neural Networks has been around since the 1940s, with the first implementation happening in the early 1950s. The concept is fairly straightforward at a high level—a series of nodes, called **neurons**, are connected to one another via their **axons**, or connectors. If these terms sound familiar, it's because they were borrowed from brain cell structures with the same names, and in some ways, similar functions.

Layers of these networks are connected to one another. Generally, there is an input layer, a hidden layer, and an output layer. This structure is represented by the following diagram:

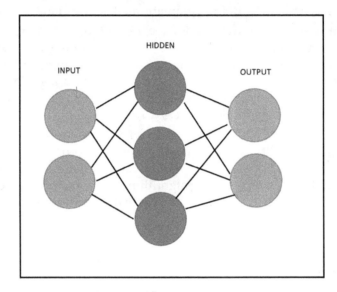

A basic neural net structure

The input, which represents the data the agent is taking in, such as images, audio, or anything else, is passed through a hidden layer, which converts the data into something the program can use and then sends that data through to the output layer for final processing.

In neural net machine learning, not all input is equal; at least, it shouldn't be. Input is weighed before being passed into the hidden layer. While it's generally okay to start with equal weights, the program can then self-adjust those weights through each iteration using back propagation. Put simply, weights are how likely the input data is to be useful in the prediction.

After many iterations of training, the AI will then be able to tackle brand new data sets, even if it has never encountered them before! While the use for machine learning in games is still limited, the field continues to expand and is a very popular topic these days. Make sure not to miss the train and check out *Machine Learning for Developers* by Rodolfo Bonnin to deep dive into all things related to machine learning.

Leveling up your game with AI

AI in games dates back all the way to the earliest games, even as far back as Namco's arcade hit Pac-Man. The AI was rudimentary at best, but even in Pac-Man, each of the enemies—Blinky, Pinky, Inky, and Clyde—had unique behaviors that challenged the player in different ways. Learning those behaviors and reacting to them adds a huge amount of depth to the game and keeps players coming back, even after over 30 years since its release.

It's the job of a good game designer to make the game challenging enough to be engaging, but not so difficult that a player can never win. To this end, AI is a fantastic tool that can help abstract the patterns that entities in games follow to make them seem more organic, alive, and real. Much like an animator through each frame or an artist through his brush, a designer or programmer can breathe life into their creations via clever use of the AI techniques covered in this book.

The role of AI in games is to make games fun by providing challenging entities to compete with, and interesting **non-player characters** (**NPCs**) that behave realistically inside the game world. The objective here is not to replicate the whole thought process of humans or animals, but merely to sell the illusion of life and make NPCs seem intelligent by having them react to the changing situations inside the game world in a way that makes sense to the player.

Technology allows us to design and create intricate patterns and behaviors, but we're not yet at the point where AI in games even begins to resemble true human behavior. While smaller, more powerful chips, buckets of memory, and even distributed computing have given programmers a much higher computational ceiling to dedicate to AI, at the end of the day, resources are still shared between other operations such as graphics rendering, physics simulation, audio processing, animation, and others, all in real time. All these systems have to play nice with each other to achieve a steady frame rate throughout the game. Like all the other disciplines in game development, optimizing AI calculations remains a huge challenge for AI developers.

Using AI in Unity

In this section, we'll walk you through some of the AI techniques being used in different types of games. We'll learn how to implement each of these features in Unity in the upcoming chapters. Unity is a flexible engine that provides a number of approaches to implement AI patterns. Some are ready to go out of the box, so to speak, while others we'll have to build from scratch. In this book, we'll focus on implementing the most essential AI patterns within Unity so that you can get your game's AI entities up and running quickly. Learning and implementing the techniques within this book will serve as a fundamental first step in the vast world of AI. Many of the concepts we will cover in this book, such as pathfinding and Navigation Meshes, are interconnected and build on top of one another. For this reason, it's important to get the fundamentals right first before digging into the high-level APIs that Unity provides.

Defining the agent

Before jumping into our first technique, we should be clear on a key term you'll see used throughout the book—the agent. An agent, as it relates to AI, is our artificially intelligent entity. When we talk about our AI, we're not specifically referring to a character, but an entity that displays complex behavior patterns, which we can refer to as non-random, or in other words, intelligent. This entity can be a character, creature, vehicle, or anything else. The agent is the autonomous entity, executing the patterns and behaviors we'll be covering. With that out of the way, let's jump in.

Finite State Machines

Finite State Machines (FSM) can be considered one of the simplest AI models, and they are commonly used in games. A state machine basically consists of a set number of states that are connected in a graph by the transitions between them. A game entity starts with an initial state and then looks out for the events and rules that will trigger a transition to another state. A game entity can only be in exactly one state at any given time.

For example, let's take a look at an AI guard character in a typical shooting game. Its states could be as simple as patrolling, chasing, and shooting:

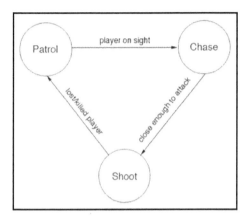

There are basically four components in a simple FSM:

- **States**: This component defines a set of distinct states that a game entity or an NPC can choose from (patrol, chase, and shoot)
- **Transitions**: This component defines relations between different states
- **Rules**: This component is used to trigger a state transition (player on sight, close enough to attack, and lost/killed player)
- **Events**: This is the component that will trigger to check the rules (guard's visible area, distance to the player, and so on)

FSMs are commonly used go-to AI patterns in game development because they are relatively easy to implement, visualize, and understand. Using simple if/else statements or switch statements, we can easily implement an FSM. It can get messy as we start to have more states and more transitions. We'll look at how to manage a simple FSM more in depth in Chapter 2, *Finite State Machines and You*.

Seeing the world through our agent's eyes

In order to make our AI convincing, our agent needs to be able to respond to the events around him, the environment, the player, and even other agents. Much like real living organisms, our agent can rely on sight, sound, and other "physical" stimuli. However, we have the advantage of being able to access much more data within our game than a real organism can from their surroundings, such as the player's location, regardless of whether or not they are in the vicinity, their inventory, the location of items around the world, and any variable you chose to expose to that agent in your code:

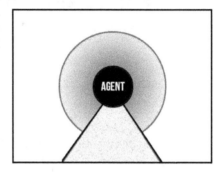

In the preceding diagram, our agent's field of vision is represented by the cone in front of it, and its hearing range is represented by the grey circle surrounding it:

Vision, sound, and other senses can be thought of, at their most essential level, as data. Vision is just light particles, sound is just vibrations, and so on. While we don't need to replicate the complexity of a constant stream of light particles bouncing around and entering our agent's eyes, we can still model the data in a way that produces believable results.

As you might imagine, we can similarly model other sensory systems, and not just the ones used for biological beings such as sight, sound, or smell, but even digital and mechanical systems that can be used by enemy robots or towers, for example sonar and radar.

If you've ever played *Metal Gear Solid*, then you've definitely seen these concepts in action—an enemy's field of vision is denoted on the player's mini map as cone-shaped fields of view. Enter the cone and an exclamation mark appears over the enemy's head, followed by an unmistakable chime, letting the player know that they've been spotted.

Path following and steering

Sometimes, we want our AI characters to roam around in the game world, following a roughly-guided or thoroughly-defined path. For example, in a racing game, the AI opponents need to navigate the road. In an RTS game, your units need to be able to get from wherever they are to the location you tell them navigating through the terrain and around each other.

To appear intelligent, our agents need to be able to determine where they are going, and if they can reach that point, they should be able to route the most efficient path and modify that path if an obstacle appears as they navigate. As you'll learn in later chapters, even path following and steering can be represented via a finite state machine. You will then see how these systems begin to tie in.

In this book, we will cover the primary methods of pathfinding and navigation, starting with our own implementation of an **A* Pathfinding System**, followed by an overview of Unity's built-in **Navigation Mesh** (**NavMesh**) feature.

Dijkstra's algorithm

While perhaps not quite as popular as A* Pathfinding (which we will cover next), it's crucial to understand Dijkstra's algorithm, as it lays the foundation for other similar approaches to finding the shortest path between two nodes in a graph. The algorithm was published by *Edsger W. Dijkstra* in 1959. Dijkstra was a computer scientist, and though he may be best known for his namesake algorithm, he also had a hand in developing other important computing concepts, such as the semaphore. It might be fair to say Dijkstra probably didn't have *StarCraft* in mind when developing his algorithm, but the concepts translate beautifully to game AI programming and remain relevant to this day.

So what does the algorithm actually *do*? In a nutshell, it computes the shortest path between two nodes along a graph by assigning a value to each connected node based on distance. The starting node is given a value of zero. As the algorithm traverses through a list of connected nodes that have not been visited, it calculates the distance to it and assigns the value to that node. If the node had already been assigned a value in a prior iteration of the loop, it keeps the smallest value. The algorithm then selects the connected node with the smallest distance value, and marks the previously selected node as *visited*, so it will no longer be considered. The process repeats until all nodes have been visited. With this information, you can then calculate the shortest path.

Need help wrapping your head around Dijkstra's algorithm? The
University of San Francisco has created a handy visualization
tool: ;https://www.cs.usfca.edu/~galles/visualization/Dijkstra.
html.

While Dijkstra's algorithm is perfectly capable, variants of it have been developed that can
solve the problem more efficiently. A* is one such algorithm, and it's one of the most widely
used pathfinding algorithms in games, due to its speed advantage over Dijkstra's original
version.

Using A* Pathfinding

There are many games in which you can find monsters or enemies that follow the player, or
go to a particular point while avoiding obstacles. For example, let's take a typical RTS game.
You can select a group of units and click on a location you want them to move to, or click on
the enemy units to attack them. Your units then need to find a way to reach the goal
without colliding with the obstacles or avoid them as intelligently as possible. The enemy
units also need to be able to do the same. Obstacles could be different for different units,
terrain, or other in-game entities. For example, an air force unit might be able to pass over a
mountain, while the ground or artillery units need to find a way around it. A* (pronounced
"A star") is a pathfinding algorithm that is widely used in games because of its performance
and accuracy. Let's take a look at an example to see how it works. Let's say we want our
unit to move from point A to point B, but there's a wall in the way and it can't go straight
towards the target. So, it needs to find a way to get to point B while avoiding the wall. The
following figure illustrates this scenario:

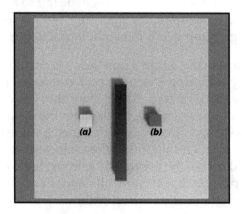

In order to find the path from point A to point B, we need to know more about the map, such as the position of the obstacles. To do this, we can split our whole map into small tiles, representing the whole map in a grid format. The tiles can also be other shapes such as hexagons and triangles. Representing the whole map in a grid makes the search area more simplified, and this is an important step in pathfinding. We can now reference our map in a small 2D array:

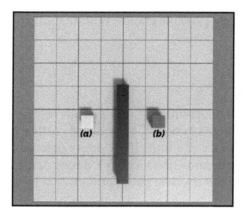

Once our map is represented by a set of tiles, we can start searching for the best path to reach the target by calculating the movement score of each tile adjacent to the starting tile, which is a tile on the map not occupied by an obstacle, and then choosing the tile with the lowest cost. We'll dive into the specifics of how we assign scores and traverse the grid in Chapter 3, *Finding Your Way*, but this is the concept of A* Pathfinding in a nutshell:

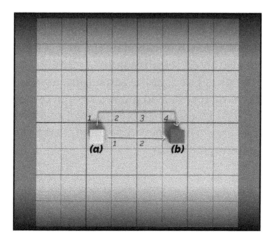

A* Pathfinding calculates the cost to move across the tiles

A* is an important pattern to know when it comes to pathfinding, but Unity also gives us a couple of features right out of the box, such as automatic Navigation Mesh generation and the NavMesh agent, which we'll explore in the next section and then in more detail in `Chapter 3`, *Finding Your Way*. These features make implementing pathfinding in your games a walk in the park (no pun intended). Whether you choose to implement your own A* solution or simply go with Unity's built-in NavMesh feature will depend on your project's needs. Each option has its own pros and cons, but ultimately, knowing about both will allow you to make the best possible choice. With that said, let's have a quick look at NavMesh.

IDA* Pathfinding

IDA* star stands for iterative deepening A*. It is a depth-first permutation of A* with a lower overall memory cost, but is generally considered costlier in terms of time. Whereas A* keeps multiple nodes in memory at a time, IDA* does not since it is a depth-first search. For this reason, IDA* may visit the same node multiple times, leading to a higher time cost. Either solution will give you the shortest path between two nodes.

In instances where the graph is too big for A* in terms of memory, IDA* is preferable, but it is generally accepted that A* is *good enough* for most use cases in games. That said, we'll explore both solutions in `Chapter 4`, *Finding Your Way*, so you can arrive at your own conclusion and pick the right pathfinding algorithm for your game.

Using Navigation Mesh

Now that we've taken a brief look at A*, let's look at some possible scenarios where we might find NavMesh a fitting approach to calculate the grid. One thing that you might notice is that using a simple grid in A* requires quite a number of computations to get a path that is the shortest to the target and, at the same time, avoids the obstacles. So, to make it cheaper and easier for AI characters to find a path, people came up with the idea of using waypoints as a guide to move AI characters from the start point to the target point. Let's say we want to move our AI character from point A to point B and we've set up three waypoints, as shown in the following figure:

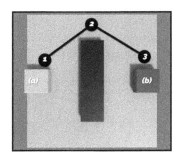

All we have to do now is to pick up the nearest waypoint and then follow its connected node leading to the target waypoint. Most games use waypoints for pathfinding because they are simple and quite effective in terms of using less computation resources. However, they do have some issues. What if we want to update the obstacles in our map? We'll also have to place waypoints for the updated map again, as shown in the following figure:

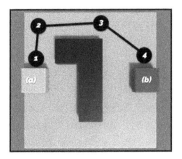

Having to manually alter waypoints every time the layout of your level changes can be cumbersome and very time-consuming. In addition, following each node to the target can mean that the AI character moves in a series of straight lines from node to node. Look at the preceding figures; it's quite likely that the AI character will collide with the wall where the path is close to the wall. If that happens, our AI will keep trying to go through the wall to reach the next target, but it won't be able to and will get stuck there. Even though we can smooth out the path by transforming it to a spline and doing some adjustments to avoid such obstacles, the problem is that the waypoints don't give us any information about the environment, other than the spline being connected between the two nodes. What if our smoothed and adjusted path passes the edge of a cliff or bridge? The new path might not be a safe path anymore. So, for our AI entities to be able to effectively traverse the whole level, we're going to need a tremendous number of waypoints, which will be really hard to implement and manage.

This is a situation where a NavMesh makes the most sense. NavMesh is another graph structure that can be used to represent our world, similar to the way we did with our square tile-based grid or waypoints graph, as shown in the following diagram:

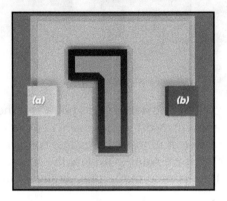

A Navigation Mesh uses convex polygons to represent the areas in the map that an AI entity can travel to. The most important benefit of using a Navigation Mesh is that it gives a lot more information about the environment than a waypoint system. Now we can adjust our path safely because we know the safe region in which our AI entities can travel. Another advantage of using a Navigation Mesh is that we can use the same mesh for different types of AI entities. Different AI entities can have different properties such as size, speed, and movement abilities. A set of waypoints is tailored for humans; AI may not work nicely for flying creatures or AI-controlled vehicles. These might need different sets of waypoints. Using a Navigation Mesh can save a lot of time in such cases.

Generating a Navigation Mesh programmatically based on a scene can be a somewhat complicated process. Fortunately, Unity 3.5 introduced a built-in Navigation Mesh generator as a pro-only feature, but is now included for free from the Unity 5 personal edition onwards. Unity's implementation provides a lot of additional functionality out of the box. Not just the generation of the NavMesh itself, but agent collision and pathfinding on the generated graph (via A*, of course) as well. Chapter 4, *Finding Your Way*, will look at some of the useful and interesting ways we can use Unity's NavMesh feature in our games, and will explore the additions and improvements that came with Unity 2017.1.

Flocking and crowd dynamics

In nature, we can observe what we refer to as flocking behavior in several species. Flocking simply refers to a group moving in unison. Schools of fish, flocks of sheep, and cicada swarms are fantastic examples of this behavior. Modeling this behavior using manual means, such as animation, can be very time-consuming and is not very dynamic. In Chapter 5, *Flocks and Crowds*, we'll explore a dynamic and programmatic approach to modeling this behavior in a believable way, using a simple set of rules that will drive the behavior of the group and each individual in a group relative to its surroundings.

Similarly, crowds of humans, be it on foot or in vehicles, can be modeled by representing the entire crowd as an entity rather than trying to model each individual as its own agent. Each individual in the group only really needs to know where the group is heading and what their nearest neighbor is up to in order to function as part of the system.

Behavior trees

The behavior tree is another pattern used to represent and control the logic behind AI agents. Behavior trees have become popular for applications in AAA games such as *Halo* and *Spore*. Previously, we briefly covered FSMs. They provide a very simple yet efficient way to define the possible behaviors of an agent, based on the different states and transitions between them. However, FSMs are considered difficult to scale as they can get unwieldy fairly quickly and require a fair amount of manual setup. We need to add many states and hardwire many transitions in order to support all the scenarios we want our agent to consider. So, we need a more scalable approach when dealing with large problems. This is where behavior trees come in.

Behavior trees are a collection of nodes organized in a hierarchical order, in which nodes are connected to parents rather than states connected to each other, resembling branches on a tree, hence the name.

The basic elements of behavior trees are task nodes, whereas states are the main elements for FSMs. There are a few different tasks such as Sequence, Selector, and Parallel Decorator. It can be a bit daunting to track what they all do. The best way to understand this is to look at an example. Let's break the following transitions and states down into tasks, as shown in the following figure:

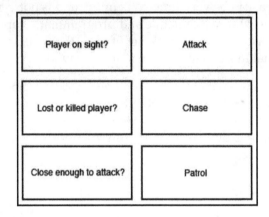

Let's look at a Selector task for this behavior tree. Selector tasks are represented by a circle with a question mark inside. The selector will evaluate each child in order, from left to right. First, it'll choose to attack the player; if the **Attack** task returns a success, the Selector task is done and will go back to the parent node, if there is one. If the **Attack** task fails, it'll try the **Chase** task. If the **Chase** task fails, it'll try the **Patrol** task. The following figure shows the basic structure of this tree concept:

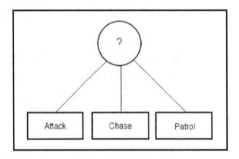

Test is one of the tasks in the behavior tree. The following diagram shows the use of Sequence tasks, denoted by a rectangle with an arrow inside it. The root selector may choose the first Sequence action. This Sequence action's first task is to check whether the player character is close enough to attack. If this task succeeds, it'll proceed with the next task, which is to attack the player. If the **Attack** task also returns successfully, the whole sequence will return as a success, and the selector will be done with this behavior and will not continue with other Sequence tasks. If the proximity check task fails, the Sequence action will not proceed to the **Attack** task, and will return a failed status to the parent selector task. Then the selector will choose the next task in the sequence, **Lost or Killed Player?** The following figure demonstrates this sequence:

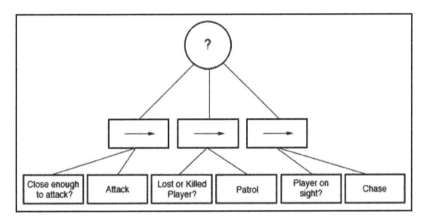

The other two common components are parallel tasks and decorators. A parallel task will execute all of its child tasks at the same time, while the Sequence and Selector tasks only execute their child tasks one by one. Decorator is another type of task that has only one child. It can change the behavior of its own child's tasks including whether to run its child's task or not, how many times it should run, and so on. We'll study how to implement a basic behavior tree system in Unity in Chapter 6, *Behavior Trees*.

Thinking with fuzzy logic

Finally, we arrive at fuzzy logic. Put simply, fuzzy logic refers to approximating outcomes as opposed to arriving at binary conclusions. We can use fuzzy logic and reasoning to add yet another layer of authenticity to our AI.

Let's use a generic bad guy soldier in a first person shooter as our agent to illustrate this basic concept. Whether we are using a finite state machine or a behavior tree, our agent needs to make decisions. Should I move to state x, y, or z? Will this task return true or false? Without fuzzy logic, we'd look at a binary value (true or false, or 0 or 1) to determine the answers to those questions. For example, can our soldier see the player? That's a yes/no binary condition. However, if we abstract the decision-making process even further, we can make our soldier behave in much more interesting ways. Once we've determined that our soldier can see the player, the soldier can then "ask" itself whether it has enough ammo to kill the player, or enough health to survive being shot at, or whether there are other allies around it to assist in taking the player down. Suddenly, our AI becomes much more interesting, unpredictable, and more believable.

This added layer of decision making is achieved by using fuzzy logic, which in the simplest terms, boils down to seemingly arbitrary or vague terminology that our wonderfully complex brains can easily assign meaning to, such as "hot" versus "warm" or "cool" versus "cold," converting this to a set of values that a computer can easily understand. In Chapter 7, *Using Fuzzy Logic to Make Your AI Seem Alive*, we'll dive deeper into how you can use fuzzy logic in your game.

Summary

Game AI and academic AI have different objectives. Academic AI researchers try to solve real-world problems and prove a theory without much limitation in terms of resources. Game AI focuses on building NPCs within limited resources that seem to be intelligent to the player. The objective of AI in games is to provide a challenging opponent that makes the game more fun to play.

We learned briefly about the different AI techniques that are widely used in games such as FSMs, sensor and input systems, flocking and crowd behaviors, path following and steering behaviors, AI path finding, Navigation Meshes, behavior trees, and fuzzy logic.

In the following chapters, we'll look at fun and relevant ways you can apply these concepts to make your game more fun. We'll start off right away in Chapter 2, *Finite State Machines and You*, with our own implementation of an FSM, and we'll dive into the concepts of agents and states and how they are applied to games.

2
Finite State Machines and You

In this chapter, we'll expand our knowledge of the FSM pattern and its uses in games and learn how to implement it in a simple Unity game. We will create a tank game with the sample code that comes with this book. We'll be dissecting the code and the components in this project. The topics we'll cover are as follows:

- Understanding Unity's state machine features
- Creating our own states and transitions
- Creating a sample scene using examples

Unity 5 introduced state machine behaviors, which are a generic expansion of the Mecanim animation states that were introduced in the 4.x cycle. These new state machine behaviors, however, are independent of the animation system, and we will learn to leverage these new features to quickly implement a state-based AI system.

In our game, the player will be able to control a tank. The enemy tanks will be moving around in the scene with reference to four waypoints. Once the player tank enters their visible range, they will start chasing us, and once they are close enough to attack, they'll start shooting at our tank agent. This simple example will be a fun way to get our feet wet in the world of AI and state FSMs.

Technical Requirements

You will be required to have Unity 2017 installed on a system that has either Windows 7 SP1+, 8, 10, 64-bit versions or Mac OS X 10.9+. The code in this book will not run on Windows XP and Vista, and server versions of Windows and OS X are not tested.

The code files of this chapter can be found on GitHub:
`https://github.com/PacktPublishing/Unity-2017-Game-AI-Programming-Third-Edition/tree/master/Chapter02`

Check out the following video to see the code in action:
`https://goo.gl/U77ytD`

Finding uses for FSMs

Although we will primarily focus on using FSMs to implement AI in our game to make it more fun and interesting, it is important to point out that FSMs are widely used throughout game and software design and programming. In fact, the system in Unity 2017 that we'll be using was first introduced in the Mecanim animation system.

We can categorize many things into states in our daily lives. The most effective patterns in programming are those that mimic the simplicity of real-life designs, and FSMs are no different. Take a look around and you'll most likely notice a number of things in one of any number of possible states. For example, is there a light bulb nearby? A light bulb can be in one of two states—on or off (so long as we're not talking about one of those fancy dimming lights). Let's go back to grade school for a moment and think about the time when we were learning about the different states matter can be in. Water, for example, can be solid, liquid, or gas. Just as in the FSM pattern in programming where variables can trigger a state change, water's transition from one state to another is caused by heat:

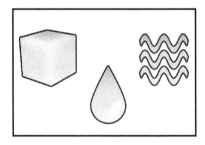

The three distinct states of water

Though there are no hard rules beyond those of our own implementation in programming design patterns, it is a characteristic of FSMs to be in one, and only one, state at any given time. With that said, transitions allow for a "hand-off", of sorts, between two states, just like ice slowly melts into water. Additionally, an agent can have multiple FSMs, driving any number of behaviors, and states can even contain state machines of their own—think Christopher Nolan's *Inception*, but with state machines instead of dreams.

There are many different implementations and variants of the FSM in C# and Unity, many of which can be found in the Unity Asset Store, but they share a few key features:

- They define the various states that an object can be in
- They provide a mechanism for transitioning from one state to another
- They provide a way to define the rules that govern transitions

Unity's Mecanim system, though intended originally for driving animations in a state-based manner, fits the bill quite well as it provides a lesser-known, more generic set of FSM features.

Creating state machine behaviors

Now that we're familiar with the concept of a state machine, let's get our hands dirty and start implementing our very own.

As of Unity 2017.1, state machines are still part of the animation system, but worry not, they are flexible and no animations are actually required to implement them. Don't be alarmed or confused if you see code referencing the `Animator` component or the `AnimationController` asset as it's merely a quirk of the current implementation. It's possible that Unity will address this in a later version, but the concepts will likely not change.

Let's fire up Unity, create a new project, and get to it.

Creating the AnimationController asset

The `AnimationController` asset is a type of asset within Unity that handles states and transitions. It is, in essence, an FSM, but it also does much more. We'll focus on the FSM portion of its functionality. An animator controller can be created from the **Assets** menu, as shown in the following image:

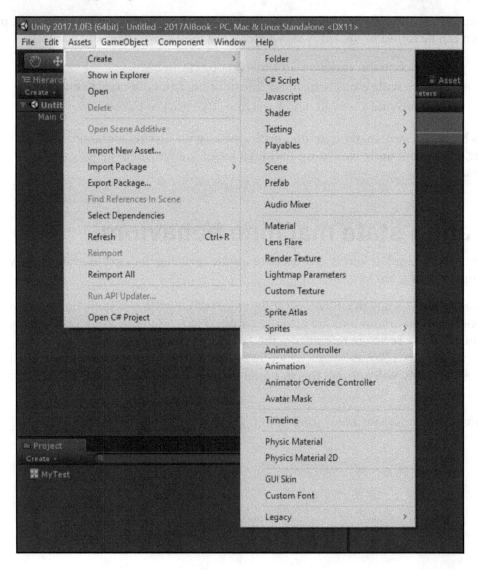

Once you create the animator controller, it will pop up in your project assets folder, ready to be named. We'll name it `TankFsm`. When you select the animator controller, unlike most other asset types, the hierarchy is blank. That is because animation controllers use their own window. You can simply click on **Open** in the hierarchy to open up the **Animator** window, or open it in the **Window** menu, as you can see in the following screenshot:

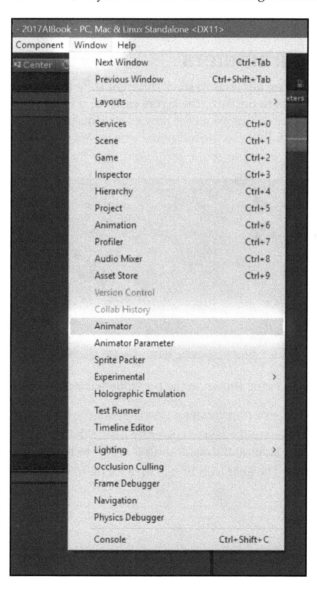

Be sure to select **Animator** and not **Animation** as these are two different windows and features entirely.

Let's familiarize ourselves with this window before moving forward.

Layers and parameters

Layers, as the name implies, allow us to stack different state machine levels on top of each other. This panel allows us to organize the layers easily and have a visual representation. We will not be doing much in this panel for now as it primarily relates to animation, but it's good to be familiar with it. Refer to the following screenshot of the window to find your way around the layers:

Here is a summary of the items shown in the previous screenshot:

- **Add layer**: The + button creates a new layer at the bottom of the list.
- **Layer list**: These are the layers currently inside the animator controller. You can click to select a layer and drag and drop layers to rearrange them.
- **Layer settings**: The gear icon brings up a menu to edit animation-specific settings for the layer.

Second, we have the **Parameters** panel, which is far more relevant to our use of the animator controller. Parameters are variables that determine when to transition between states, and we can access them via scripts to drive our states. There are four types of parameters—float, int, bool, and trigger. You should already be familiar with the first three as they are primitive types in C#, but trigger is specific to the animator controller, not to be confused with physics triggers, which do not apply here. Triggers are just a means to trigger a transition between states explicitly.

The following screenshot shows the elements in the **Parameters** panel:

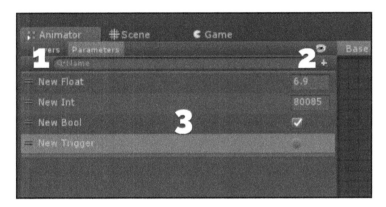

Here is a summary of the items depicted in the previous screenshot:

- **Search**: We can quickly search through our parameters here. Simply type in the name and the list will populate with the search results.
- **Add parameter**: This button lets you add new parameters. When you click on it, you must select the parameter type.
- **Parameter list**: This is the list of parameters you've created. You can assign and view their values here. You can also reorder the parameters to your liking by dragging and dropping them in the correct order. This is merely for organization and does not affect functionality at all.

Lastly, there is an eyeball icon, which you can click to hide the **Layers** and **Parameters** panels altogether. When the panels are closed, you can still create new layers by clicking on the **Layers** dropdown and selecting **Create New Layer**:

The animation controller inspector

The animation controller inspector is slightly different from the regular inspector found throughout Unity. While the regular inspector allows you to add components to the game objects, the animation controller inspector has a button labeled **Add Behaviour**, which allows you to add a StateMachineBehaviour to it. This is the main distinction between the two types of inspectors, but apart from this, it will display the serialized information for any selected state, substate, transition, or blend tree, just as the regular inspector displays the data for the selected game object and its components.

Bringing behaviors into the picture

State machine behaviors are a unique, new concept in Unity 5. While states existed, conceptually, in the original implementation of Mecanim, transitions were handled behind the scenes and you did not have much control over what happened upon entering, transitioning, or exiting a state. Unity 5 addressed this issue by introducing behaviors; they provide the built-in functionality to handle typical FSM logic.

Behaviors are sly and tricky. Though their name might lead you to believe they are related to MonoBehaviour, do not fall for it; if anything, these two are distant cousins at best. In fact, behaviors derive from ScriptableObject, not MonoBehaviour, so they exist only as assets, which cannot be placed in a scene or added as components to a GameObject.

Creating our very first state

Okay, so the header is not entirely true since Unity creates a few default states for us in our animator controller—**New State**, **Any State**, **Entry**, and **Exit**—but let's just agree that those don't count for now, okay? Let's take a look at some of the things we can do in our newly-created animation controller:

- You can select states in this window by clicking on them, and you can move them by dragging and dropping them anywhere in the canvas.
- Select the state named **New State** and delete it by either right-clicking and then clicking on **Delete** or simply hitting the *Delete* key on your keyboard.
- If you select the **Any State** state, you'll notice that you do not have the option to delete it. The same is true for the **Entry** state. These are required states in an animator controller and have unique uses, which we'll cover up ahead:

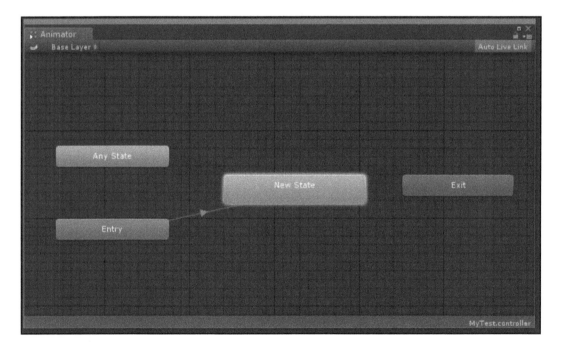

To create our (true) first state, right-click anywhere on the canvas and then select **Create State**, which opens up a few options, from which we'll select **Empty**. The other two options, **From Selected Clip** and **From New Blend Tree**, are not immediately applicable to our project, so we'll skip these. Now we've officially created our first state.

Transitioning between states

You'll notice that upon creating our state, an arrow is created connecting the **Entry** state to it, and that its node is orange. Unity will automatically set default states to look orange to differentiate them from other states. When you only have one state, it is automatically selected as the default state, and as such, it is automatically connected to the entry state. You can manually select which state is the default state by right-clicking on it and then clicking on **Set as Layer Default State**. It will then become orange, and the entry state will automatically connect itself to it. The connecting arrow is a **transition connector**. Transition connectors allow us some control over how and when the transition occurs, but the connector from the entry state to the default state is unique in that it does not provide us with any options, since this transition happens automatically.

You can manually assign transitions between states by right-clicking on a state node and then selecting **Make Transition**. This will create a transition arrow from the state you selected to your mouse cursor. To select the destination of the transition, simply click on the destination node and that's it. Note that you cannot redirect the transitions though. We can only hope that the kind folks behind Unity add that functionality at a later point, but for now, you must remove a transition by selecting it and deleting it, and then assigning an all-new transition manually.

Setting up our player tank

Open up the sample project included with this book for this chapter.

It is a good idea to group similar assets together in your project folder to keep them organized. For example, you can group your state machines in a folder called `StateMachines`. The assets provided for this chapter are grouped for you already, so you can drop the assets and scripts you create during this chapter into the corresponding folder.

Creating the enemy tank

Let's go ahead and create an animator controller in your assets folder. This will be your enemy tank's state machine. Call it `EnemyFsm`.

This state machine will drive the tank's basic actions. As described earlier in our example, the enemy can patrol, chase, and shoot the player. Let's go ahead and set up our state machine. Select the `EnemyFsm` asset and open up the **Animator** window.

Now, we'll go ahead and create three empty states that will conceptually and functionally represent our enemy tank's states. Name them `Patrol`, `Chase`, and `Shoot`. Once they are created and named, we'll want to make sure we have the correct default state assigned. At the moment, this will vary depending on the order in which you created and named the states, but we want the **Patrol** state to be the default state, so right-click on it and select **Set as Layer Default State**. Now it is colored orange and the **Entry** state is connected to it.

Choosing transitions

At this point, we have to make some design and logic decisions regarding the way our states will flow into each other. When we map out these transitions, we also want to keep in mind the conditions that trigger the transitions to make sure they are logical and work from a design-standpoint. Out in the wild, when you're applying these techniques on your own, different factors will play into how these transitions are handled. In order to best illustrate the topic at hand, we'll keep our transitions simple and logical:

- **Patrol**: From patrol, we can transition into chasing. We will use a chain of conditions to choose which state we'll transition into, if any. Can the enemy tank see the player? If yes, we go to the next step; if not, we continue with patrolling.
- **Chase**: From this state, we'll want to continue to check whether the player is within sight to continue chasing, close enough to shoot, or completely out of sight—that would send us back into the **Patrol** state.
- **Shoot**: As earlier, we'll want to check our range for shooting and then the line of sight to determine whether or not we can chase to get within the range.

This particular example has a simple and clean set of transition rules. If we connect our states accordingly, we'll end up with a graph looking more or less similar to this one:

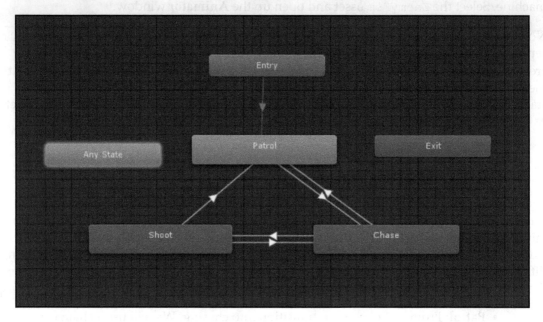

Keep in mind that the placement of the nodes is entirely up to you, and it does not affect the functionality of the state machine in any way. You can try to place your nodes in a way that keeps them organized so that you can track your transitions visually.

Now that we have our states mapped out, let's assign some behaviors to them.

Making the cogs turn

This is the part I'm sure you've been waiting for. I know, I've kept you waiting, but for good reason. As we now get ready to dive into the coding, we do so with a good understanding of the logical connection between the states in our FSM. Without further ado, select our **Patrol** state. In the hierarchy, you'll see a button labeled **Add Behaviour**. Clicking this gives you a context menu very similar to the **Add Component** button on regular game objects, but as we mentioned before, this button creates the oh-so-unique state machine behaviors.

Go ahead and name this behavior `TankPatrolState`. Doing so creates a script of the same name in your project and attaches it to the state we created it from. You can open this script via the project window, or by double-clicking on the name of the script in the inspector. What you'll find inside will look similar to this:

```
using UnityEngine;
using System.Collections;

public class TankPatrolState : StateMachineBehaviour {

    // OnStateEnter is called when a transition starts and the state machine
    starts to evaluate this state
    //override public void OnStateEnter(Animator animator, AnimatorStateInfo
    stateInfo, int layerIndex) {
    //
    //}

    // OnStateUpdate is called on each Update frame between OnStateEnter and
    OnStateExit callbacks
    //override public void OnStateUpdate(Animator animator,
    AnimatorStateInfo stateInfo, int layerIndex) {
    //
    //}

    // OnStateExit is called when a transition ends and the state machine
    finishes evaluating this state
    //override public void OnStateExit(Animator animator, AnimatorStateInfo
    stateInfo, int layerIndex) {
    //
    //}

    // OnStateMove is called right after Animator.OnAnimatorMove(). Code
    that processes and affects root motion should be implemented here
    //override public void OnStateMove(Animator animator, AnimatorStateInfo
    stateInfo, int layerIndex) {
    //
    //}

    // OnStateIK is called right after Animator.OnAnimatorIK(). Code that
    sets up animation IK (inverse kinematics) should be implemented here.
    //override public void OnStateIK(Animator animator, AnimatorStateInfo
    stateInfo, int layerIndex) {
    //
    //}
}
```

Downloading the example code

You can download the example code files from your account at `http://www.packtpub.com` for all the Packt Publishing books you have purchased. If you purchased this book elsewhere, you can visit `http://www.packtpub.com/support` and register to have the files e-mailed directly to you.

Before we begin, uncomment each method. Let's break it down step by step. Unity creates this file for you, but all the methods are commented out. Essentially, the commented code acts as a guide. Much like the methods provided for you in a `MonoBehaviour`, these methods are called for you by the underlying logic. You don't need to know what's going on behind the scenes to use them; you simply have to know when they are called to leverage them. Luckily, the commented code provides a brief description of when each method is called, and the names are fairly descriptive themselves. There are two methods here we don't need to worry about, `OnStateIK` and `OnStateMove`, which are animation messages, so go ahead and delete them and save the file.

To reiterate what's stated in the code's comments, the following things happen:

- `OnStateEnter` is called when you enter the state, as soon as the transition starts
- `OnStateUpdate` is called on each frame, after the `MonoBehaviors` update
- `OnStateExit` is called after the transition out of the state is finished

The following two states, as we mentioned, are animation-specific, so we do not use those for our purposes:

- `OnStateIK` is called just before the IK system gets updated; this is an animation and rig-specific concept
- `OnStateMove` is used on avatars that are set up to use root motion

Another important piece of information to note is the parameters passed into these methods:

- The `animator` parameter is a reference to the animator that contains this animator controller, and therefore this state machine. By extension, you can fetch a reference to the game object that the animator controller is on, and from there, you can grab any other components attached to it. Remember, the state machine behavior exists only as an asset, and does not exist in the class, meaning this is the best way to get references to runtime classes, such as mono behaviors.
- The animator state info provides information about the state you're currently in; however, the uses for this are primarily focused on animation state information, so it's not as useful for our application.
- Lastly, we have the layer index, which is an integer telling us which layer within the state machine our state is in. The base layer is index zero, and each layer above that is a higher number.

Now that we understand the basics of state machine behavior, let's get the rest of our components in order. Before we can actually see these behaviors in action, we have to go back to our state machine and add some parameters that will drive the states.

Setting conditions

We will need to provide our enemy tank with a few conditions to transitions states. These are the actual parameters that will drive the functionality.

Let's begin with the **Patrol** state. In order for our enemy tank to go from **Patrol** to **Shoot**, we need to be in range of the player; in other words, we'll be checking the distance between the enemy and the player, which is best represented by a float value. So, in your **Parameters** panel, add a float and name it `distanceFromPlayer`. We can also use this parameter to determine whether or not to go into the **Chase** state.

The **Shoot** state and the **Chase** state will share a common condition, which is whether or not the player is visible. We'll determine this via a simple raycast, which will, in turn, tell us whether the player was in the line of sight or not. The best parameter for this is a Boolean, so create a Boolean and call it `isPlayerVisible`. Leave the parameter unchecked, which means false.

Now we'll assign the conditions via the transition connectors' inspector. To do this, simply select a connector. When selected, the inspector will display some information about the current transition and, most importantly, the conditions, which show up as a list. To add a condition, simply click on the + (plus) sign:

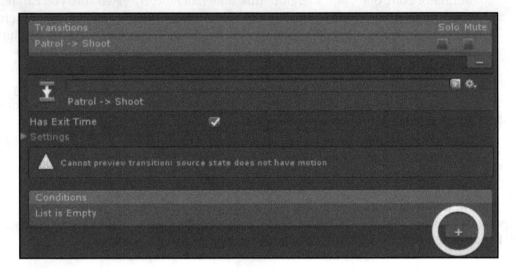

Let's tackle each transition one by one:

- **Patrol** to **Chase**
    - **distanceFromPlayer < 5**
    - **isPlayerVisible == true**

The Patrol to Chase transition conditions

Chase to patrol gets a bit more interesting as we have two *separate* conditions that can trigger a transition. If we were to simply add two conditions to that transition, both would have to be evaluated to true in order for the transition to occur. But we want to check whether the player is out of range or out of sight. Luckily, we can have multiple transitions between the same two states. Simply add another transition connection as you normally would. Right-click on the **Chase** state and then make a transition to the **Patrol** state. You'll notice that you now have two transitions listed at the top of the inspector. In addition, your transition connection indicator shows multiple arrows instead of just one to indicate that there are multiple transitions between these two states. Selecting each transition in the inspector will allow you to give each one separate conditions:

- **Chase** to **Patrol** (A)
    - distanceFromPlayer > 5
- **Chase** to **Patrol** (B)
    - isPlayerVisible == false
- **Chase** to **Shoot**
    - distanceFromPlayer < 3
    - isPlayerVisible == true
- **Shoot** to **Chase**
    - distanceFromPlayer > 3
    - distanceFromPlayer < 5
    - isPlayerVisible == true
- **Shoot** to **Patrol** (A)
    - distanceFromPlayer > 6
- **Shoot** to **Patrol** (B)
    - isPlayerVisible == false

We now have our states and transitions set. Next, we need to create the script that will drive these values. All we need to do is set the values, and the state machine will handle the rest.

Driving parameters via code

Before going any further, we'll need a few things from the assets we imported earlier in the chapter. For starters, go ahead and open the DemoScene for this chapter. You'll notice the scene is fairly stripped down and only contains an environment prefab and some waypoint transforms. Go ahead and drop the EnemyTankPlaceholder prefab into the scene.

You may notice a few components that you may or may not be familiar with on the `EnemyTank`. We'll get a chance to thoroughly explore `NavMesh` and `NavMeshAgent` in Chapter 4, *Finding Your Way*, but for now, these are necessary components to make the whole thing work. What you will want to focus on is the `Animator` component which will house the state machine (animator controller) we created earlier. Go ahead and drop the state machine into the empty slot before continuing.

We will also need a placeholder for the player. Go ahead and drop in the `PlayerTankPlaceholder` prefab as well. We won't be doing much with this for now. As with the enemy tank placeholder prefab, the player tank placeholder prefab has a few components that we can ignore for now. Simply place it in the scene and continue.

Next, you'll want to add a new component to the `EnemyTankPlaceholder` game object—the `TankAi.cs` script, which is located in the Chapter 2 scripts folder. If we open up the script, we'll find this inside it:

```
using UnityEngine;
using System.Collections;

public class TankAi : MonoBehaviour {
    // General state machine variables
    private GameObject player;
    private Animator animator;
    private Ray ray;
    private RaycastHit hit;
    private float maxDistanceToCheck = 6.0f;
    private float currentDistance;
    private Vector3 checkDirection;

    // Patrol state variables
    public Transform pointA;
    public Transform pointB;
    public NavMeshAgent navMeshAgent;
    private int currentTarget;
    private float distanceFromTarget;
    private Transform[] waypoints = null;

    private void Awake() {
        player = GameObject.FindWithTag("Player");
        animator = gameObject.GetComponent<Animator>();
        pointA = GameObject.Find("p1").transform;
        pointB = GameObject.Find("p2").transform;
        navMeshAgent = gameObject.GetComponent<NavMeshAgent>();
        waypoints = new Transform[2] {
            pointA,
            pointB
```

```
        };
        currentTarget = 0;
        navMeshAgent.SetDestination(waypoints[currentTarget].position);
    }

    private void FixedUpdate() {
        //First we check distance from the player
        currentDistance = Vector3.Distance(player.transform.position,
transform.position);
        animator.SetFloat("distanceFromPlayer", currentDistance);

        //Then we check for visibility
        checkDirection = player.transform.position - transform.position;
        ray = new Ray(transform.position, checkDirection);
        if (Physics.Raycast(ray, out hit, maxDistanceToCheck)) {
            if(hit.collider.gameObject == player){
                animator.SetBool("isPlayerVisible", true);
            } else {
                animator.SetBool("isPlayerVisible", false);
            }
        } else {
            animator.SetBool("isPlayerVisible", false);
        }

        //Lastly, we get the distance to the next waypoint target
        distanceFromTarget =
Vector3.Distance(waypoints[currentTarget].position, transform.position);
        animator.SetFloat("distanceFromWaypoint", distanceFromTarget);
    }

    public void SetNextPoint() {
        switch (currentTarget) {
            case 0:
                currentTarget = 1;
                break;
            case 1:
                currentTarget = 0;
                break;
        }
        navMeshAgent.SetDestination(waypoints[currentTarget].position);
    }
}
```

We have a series of variables that are required to run this script, so we'll run through what they're for in order:

- `GameObject player`: This is a reference to the player placeholder prefab we dropped in earlier.
- `Animator animator`: This is the animator for our enemy tank, which contains the state machine we created.
- `Ray ray`: This is simply a declaration for a ray that we'll use in a raycast test on our `FixedUpdate` loop.
- `RaycastHit hit`: This is a declaration for the hit information we'll receive from our raycast test.
- `Float maxDistanceToCheck`: This number coincides with the value we set in our transitions inside the state machine earlier. Essentially, we are saying that we're only checking as far as this distance for the player. Beyond that, we can assume that the player is out of range.
- `Float currentDistance`: This is the current distance between the player and the enemy tanks.

You'll notice we skipped a few variables. Don't worry, we'll come back to cover these later. These are the variables we'll be using for our **Patrol** state.

Our `Awake` method handles fetching the references to our player and animator variables. You can also declare the preceding variables as public or prefix them with the `[SerializeField]` attribute and set them via the inspector.

The `FixedUpdate` method is fairly straightforward; the first part gets the distance between the position of the player and the enemy tank. The part to pay special attention to is `animator.SetFloat("distanceFromPlayer", currentDistance)`, which passes the information from this script into the parameter we defined earlier for our state machine. The same is true for the preceding section of the code, which passes in the hit result of the raycast as a Boolean. Lastly, it sets the `distanceFromTarget` variable, which we'll be using for the **Patrol** state in the next section.

As you can see, none of the code concerns itself with how or why the state machine will handle transitions; it merely passes in the information the state machine needs, and the state machine handles the rest. Pretty cool, right?

Making our enemy tank move

You may have noticed in addition to the variables we didn't cover yet, that our tank has no logic in place for moving. This can be easily handled with a substate machine, which is a state machine within a state. This may sound confusing at first, but we can easily break down the **Patrol** state into substates. In our example, the **Patrol** state will be in one of the two substates—moving to the current waypoint or finding the next waypoint. A waypoint is essentially a destination for our agent to move toward. In order to make these changes, we'll need to go into our state machine again.

First, create a substate by clicking on an empty area on the canvas and then selecting **Create Sub-State Machine**. Since we already have our original **Patrol** state and all the connections that go with it, we can just drag and drop our **Patrol** state into our newly-created substate to merge the two. As you drag the **Patrol** state over the substate, you'll notice a plus sign appears by your cursor; this means you're adding one state to the other. When you drop the **Patrol** state in, the new substate will absorb it. Substates have a unique look: they are six-sided rather than rectangular. Go ahead and rename the substate to `Patrol`:

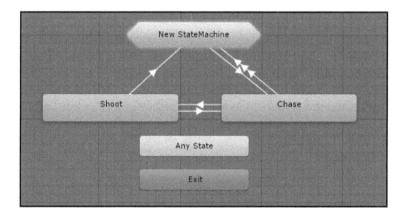

To enter a substate, simply double-click on it. Think of it as going a level lower into the substate. The window will look fairly similar, but you will notice a few things—your **Patrol** state is connected to a node called **(Up) Base Layer**, which essentially is the connection from this level to the upper level that the substate machine sits on. The **Entry** state connects directly to the **Patrol** state.

Unfortunately, this is not the functionality we want, as it's a closed loop that doesn't allow us to get in and out of the state into the individual waypoint states we need to create; so let's make some changes. First, we'll change the name of the substate to `PatrolEntry`. Next, we need to assign some transitions. When we enter this **Entry** state, we want to decide whether to continue moving to the current waypoint, or to find a new one. We'll represent each of the outcomes as a state, so create two states, `MovingToTarget` and `FindingNewTarget`, then create transitions from the **PatrolEntry** state to each one of the new states. Likewise, you'll want to create a transition between the two new states, meaning a transition from the `MovingToTarget` state to the `FindingNewTarget` state and vice versa. Now, add a new float parameter called `distanceFromWaypoint` and set up your conditions like this:

- **PatrolEntry** to **MovingToTarget**:
  - **distanceFromWaypoint** > 1
- **PatrolEntry** to **FindingNewTarget**:
  - **distanceFromWaypoint** < 1
- **MovingToTarget** to **FindingNewTarget**:
  - **distanceFromWaypoint** < 1

You're probably wondering why we didn't assign the transition rule from the **FindingNewTarget** state to the **MovingToTarget** state. This is because we'll be executing some code via state machine behavior and then automatically going into the **MovingToTarget** state without requiring any conditions. Go ahead and select the **FindingNewTarget** state and add a behavior and call it `SelectWaypointState`.

Open up the new script and remove all the methods, except for `OnStateEnter`. Add the following functionality to it:

```
TankAi tankAi = animator.gameObject.GetComponent<TankAi>();
tankAi.SetNextPoint();
```

What we're doing here is getting a reference to our `TankAi` script and calling its `SetNextPoint()` method. Simple enough, right?

Lastly, we need to redo our outgoing connections. Our new states don't have transitions out of this level, so we need to add one, using the exact same conditions that our **PatrolEntry** state has, to the **(Up) Base Layer** state. This is where **Any State** comes in handy—it allows us to transition from any state to another state, regardless of individual transition connections, so that we don't have to add transitions from each state to the **(Up) Base Layer** state; we simply add it once to the **Any State**, and we're set! Add a transition from the **Any State** to the **PatrolEntry** state and use the same conditions the **Entry** state has to the **(Up) Base Layer** state. This is a workaround for not being able to connect directly from the **Any State** to the **(Up) Base Layer** state.

When you're done, your substate machine should look similar to this:

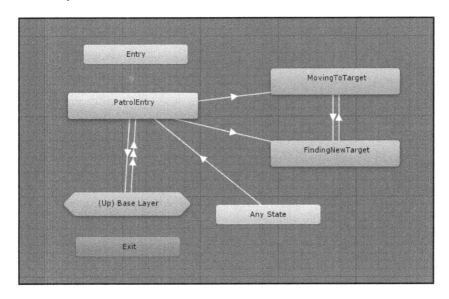

Testing

Now, all we have to do is hit play and watch our enemy tank patrol back and forth between the two provided waypoints. If we place the player in the editor, in the enemy tank's path, we'll see the transition happen in the animator, out of the **Patrol** state and into the **Chase** state, and when we move the player out of range, back into the **Patrol** state. You'll notice our **Chase** and **Shoot** states are not fully fleshed out yet. This is because we'll be implementing these states via concepts we'll cover in Chapter 3, *Implementing Sensors*, and Chapter 4, *Finding Your Way*.

Summary

In this chapter, we learned how to implement state machines in Unity 2017 using animator and controller-based state machines for what will be our tank game. We learned about state machine behaviors and transitions between states. With all of these concepts covered, we then applied the simple state machine to an agent, thus creating our first artificially intelligent entity!

In the next chapter, we'll continue to build our tank game and give our agent more complex methods for sensing the world around it.

3
Implementing Sensors

In this chapter, we'll learn to implement AI behavior using the concept of a sensory system similar to what living entities have. As we discussed earlier, a character AI system needs to have awareness of its environment such as where the obstacles are, where the enemy it is looking for is, whether the enemy is visible in the player's sight, and so on. The quality of our NPC's AI completely depends on the information it can get from the environment. Nothing breaks the level of immersion in a game like an NPC getting stuck behind a wall. Based on the information the NPC can collect, the AI system can decide which logic to execute in response to that data. If the sensory systems do not provide enough data, or the AI system is unable to properly take action on that data, the agent can begin to glitch, or behave in a way contrary to what the developer, or more importantly the player, would expect. Some games have become infamous for their comically bad AI glitches, and it's worth a quick internet search to find some videos of AI glitches for a good laugh.

We can detect all the environment parameters and check them against our predetermined values if we want. But using a proper design pattern will help us maintain code and thus will be easy to extend. This chapter will introduce a design pattern that we can use to implement sensory systems. We will be covering:

- What sensory systems are
- Some of the different sensory systems that exist
- How to set up a sample tank with sensing

Technical Requirements

You will be required to have Unity 2017 installed on a system that has either Windows 7 SP1+, 8, 10, 64-bit versions or Mac OS X 10.9+. The code in this book will not run on Windows XP and Vista, and server versions of Windows and OS X are not tested.

The code files of this chapter can be found on GitHub:
`https://github.com/PacktPublishing/Unity-2017-Game-AI-Programming-Third-Edition/tree/master/Chapter03`

Check out the following video to see the code in action:
`https://goo.gl/AkQJnY`

Basic sensory systems

Our agent's sensory systems should believably emulate real-world senses such as vision, sound, and so on, to build a model of its environment, much like we do as humans. Have you ever tried to navigate a room in the dark after shutting off the lights? It gets more and more difficult as you move from your initial position when you turned the lights off because your perspective shifts and you have to rely more and more on your fuzzy memory of the room's layout. While our senses rely on and take in a constant stream of data to navigate their environment, our agent's AI is a lot more forgiving, giving us the freedom to examine the environment at predetermined intervals. This allows us to build a more efficient system in which we can focus only on the parts of the environment that are relevant to the agent.

The concept of a basic sensory system is that there will be two components, `Aspect` and `Sense`. Our AI characters will have senses, such as perception, smell, and touch. These senses will look out for specific aspects such as enemies and bandits. For example, you could have a patrol guard AI with a perception sense that's looking for other game objects with an enemy aspect, or it could be a zombie entity with a smell sense looking for other entities with an aspect defined as a brain.

For our demo, this is basically what we are going to implement—a base interface called `Sense` that will be implemented by other custom senses. In this chapter, we'll implement perspective and touch senses. Perspective is what animals use to see the world around them. If our AI character sees an enemy, we want to be notified so that we can take some action. Likewise with touch, when an enemy gets too close, we want to be able to sense that, almost as if our AI character can hear that the enemy is nearby. Then we'll write a minimal `Aspect` class that our senses will be looking for.

Cone of sight

In the example provided in `Chapter 2`, *Finite State Machines and You*, we set up our agent to detect the player tank using line of sight, which is literally a line in the form of a raycast. A **raycast** is a feature in Unity that allows you to determine which objects are intersected by a line cast from a point toward a given direction. While this is a fairly efficient way to handle visual detection in a simple way, it doesn't accurately model the way vision works for most entities. An alternative to using line of sight is using a cone-shaped field of vision. As the following figure illustrates, the field of vision is literally modeled using a cone shape. This can be in 2D or 3D, as appropriate for your type of game:

The preceding figure illustrates the concept of a cone of sight. In this case, beginning with the source, that is, the agent's eyes, the cone grows, but becomes less accurate with distance, as represented by the fading color of the cone.

The actual implementation of the cone can vary from a basic overlap test to a more complex realistic model, mimicking eyesight. In a simple implementation, it is only necessary to test whether an object overlaps with the cone of sight, ignoring distance or periphery. A complex implementation mimics eyesight more closely; as the cone widens away from the source, the field of vision grows, but the chance of getting to see things toward the edges of the cone diminishes compared to those near the center of the source.

Hearing, feeling, and smelling using spheres

One very simple yet effective way of modeling sounds, touch, and smell is via the use of spheres. For sounds, for example, we can imagine the center as being the source and the loudness dissipating the farther from the center the listener is. Inversely, the listener can be modeled instead of, or in addition to, the source of the sound. The listener's hearing is represented by a sphere, and the sounds closest to the listener are more likely to be "heard." We can modify the size and position of the sphere relative to our agent to accommodate feeling and smelling.

The following figure represents our sphere and how our agent fits into the setup:

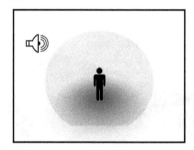

As with sight, the probability of an agent registering the sensory event can be modified, based on the distance from the sensor or as a simple overlap event, where the sensory event is always detected as long as the source overlaps the sphere.

Expanding AI through omniscience

In a nutshell, omniscience is really just a way to make your AI cheat. While your agent doesn't necessarily know everything, it simply means that they *can* know anything. In some ways, this can seem like the antithesis to realism, but often the simplest solution is the best solution. Allowing our agent access to seemingly hidden information about its surroundings or other entities in the game world can be a powerful tool to provide an extra layer of complexity.

In games, we tend to model abstract concepts using concrete values. For example, we may represent a player's health with a numeric value ranging from 0 to 100. Giving our agent access to this type of information allows it to make realistic decisions, even though having access to that information is not realistic. You can also think of omniscience as your agent being able to *use the force* or sense events in your game world without having to *physically* experience them.

While omniscience is not necessarily a specific pattern or technique, it's another tool in your toolbox as a game developer to cheat a bit and make your game more interesting by, in essence, bending the rules of AI, and giving your agent data that they may not otherwise have had access to through *physical* means.

Getting creative with sensing

While cones, spheres, and lines are among the most basic ways an agent can see, hear, and perceive their environment, they are by no means the only ways to implement these senses. If your game calls for other types of sensing, feel free to combine these patterns. Want to use a cylinder or a sphere to represent a field of vision? Go for it. Want to use boxes to represent the sense of smell? Sniff away!

Using the tools at your disposal, come up with creative ways to model sensing in terms relative to your player. Combine different approaches to create unique gameplay mechanics for your games by mixing and matching these concepts. For example, a magic-sensitive but blind creature could completely ignore a character right in front of them until they cast or receive the effect of a magic spell. Maybe certain NPCs can track the player using smell, and walking through a collider marked *water* can clear the scent from the player so that the NPC can no longer track him. As you progress through the book, you'll be given all the tools to pull these and many other mechanics off—sensing, decision-making, pathfinding, and so on. As we cover some of these techniques, start thinking about creative twists for your game.

Setting up the scene

In order to get started with implementing the sensing system, you can jump right into the example provided for this chapter, or set up the scene yourself, by following these steps:

1. Let's create a few barriers to block the line of sight from our AI character to the tank. These will be short but wide cubes grouped under an empty game object called `Obstacles`.
2. Add a plane to be used as a floor.
3. Then, we add a directional light so that we can see what is going on in our scene.

As you can see in the example, there is a target 3D model, which we use for our player, and we represent our AI agent using a simple cube. We will also have a `Target` object to show us where the tank will move to in our scene.

For simplicity, our example provides a point light as a child of the Target so that we can easily see our target destination in the game view. Our scene hierarchy will look similar to the following screenshot after you've set everything up correctly:

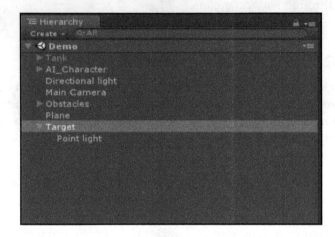

The scene hierarchy

Now we will position the tank, the AI character, and walls randomly in our scene. Increase the size of the plane to something that looks good. Fortunately, in this demo, our objects float, so nothing will fall off the plane. Also, be sure to adjust the camera so that we can have a clear view of the following scene:

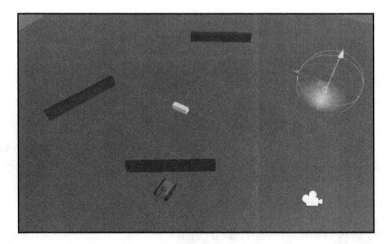

Our game scene

With the essential setup out of the way, we can begin tackling the code for driving the various systems.

Setting up the player tank and aspect

Our `Target` object is a simple sphere game object with the mesh render removed, so that we end up with only the **Sphere Collider**.

Look at the following code in the `Target.cs` file:

```
using UnityEngine;

public class Target : MonoBehaviour
{
    public Transform targetMarker;
    void Start (){}

    void Update ()
    {
        int button = 0;

        //Get the point of the hit position when the mouse is being clicked
        if(Input.GetMouseButtonDown(button))
        {
            Ray ray = Camera.main.ScreenPointToRay(Input.mousePosition);
            RaycastHit hitInfo;

            if (Physics.Raycast(ray.origin, ray.direction, out hitInfo))
            {
                Vector3 targetPosition = hitInfo.point;
                targetMarker.position = targetPosition;
            }
        }
    }
}
```

You'll notice we left in an empty `Start` method in the code. While there is a cost in having empty `Start`, `Update`, and other `MonoBehaviour` events that don't do anything, we can sometimes choose to leave the `Start` method in during development, so that the component shows an enable/disable toggle in the inspector.

Attach this script to our `Target` object, which is what we assigned in the inspector to the `targetMarker` variable. The script detects the mouse click event and then, using a raycast, it detects the mouse click point on the plane in the 3D space. After that, it updates the `Target` object to that position in the world space in the scene.

 A raycast is a feature of the Unity Physics API that shoots a virtual ray from a given origin towards a given direction, and returns data on any colliders hit along the way.

Implementing the player tank

Our player tank is the simple tank model we used in Chapter 2, *Finite State Machines and You*, with a kinematic rigid body component attached. The rigid body component is needed in order to generate trigger events whenever we do collision detection with any AI characters. The first thing we need to do is to assign the tag `Player` to our tank.

 The `isKinematic` flag in Unity's Rigidbody component makes it so that external forces are ignored, so that you can control the Rigidbody entirely from code or from an animation, while still having access to the Rigidbody API.

The tank is controlled by the `PlayerTank` script, which we will create in a moment. This script retrieves the target position on the map and updates its destination point and the direction accordingly.

The code in the `PlayerTank.cs` file is as follows:

```
using UnityEngine;

public class PlayerTank : MonoBehaviour
{
    public Transform targetTransform;
    public float targetDistanceTolerance = 3.0f;

    private float movementSpeed;
    private float rotationSpeed;

    // Use this for initialization
    void Start ()
    {
        movementSpeed = 10.0f;
        rotationSpeed = 2.0f;
```

```
    }
    // Update is called once per frame
    void Update ()
       {
            if (Vector3.Distance(transform.position, targetTransform.position)
< targetDistanceTolerance)
            {
                 return;
            }

            Vector3 targetPosition = targetTransform.position;
            targetPosition.y = transform.position.y;
            Vector3 direction = targetPosition - transform.position;

            Quaternion tarRot = Quaternion.LookRotation(direction);
            transform.rotation = Quaternion.Slerp(transform.rotation, tarRot,
rotationSpeed * Time.deltaTime);

            transform.Translate(new Vector3(0, 0, movementSpeed *
Time.deltaTime));
       }
}
```

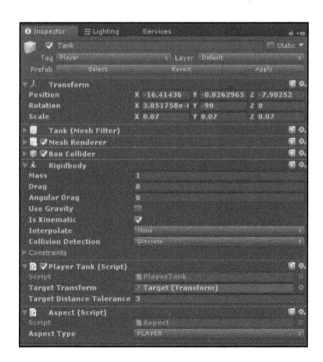

Properties of our tank object

The preceding screenshot shows us a snapshot of our script in the inspector once applied to our tank.

This script queries the position of the `Target` object on the map and updates its destination point and the direction accordingly. After we assign this script to our tank, be sure to assign our `Target` object to the `targetTransform` variable.

Implementing the Aspect class

Next, let's take a look at the `Aspect.cs` class. `Aspect` is a very simple class with just one public enum of type `AspectTypes` called `aspectType`. That's all of the variables we need in this component. Whenever our AI character senses something, we'll check the `aspectType` to see whether it's the aspect that the AI has been looking for.

The code in the `Aspect.cs` file looks like this:

```
using UnityEngine;

public class Aspect : MonoBehaviour {
  public enum AspectTypes {
    PLAYER,
    ENEMY,
  }
  public AspectTypes aspectType;
}
```

Attach this aspect script to our player tank and set the `aspectType` to PLAYER, as shown in the following screenshot:

Setting the Aspect Type of the tank

Creating an AI character

Our NPC will be roaming around the scene in a random direction. It'll have the following two senses:

- The perspective sense will check whether the tank aspect is within a set visible range and distance
- The touch sense will detect if the enemy aspect has collided with its box collider, which we'll be adding to the tank in a later step

Because our player tank will have the PLAYER aspect type, the NPC will be looking for any aspectType not equal to its own.

The code in the Wander.cs file is as follows:

```
using UnityEngine;

public class Wander : MonoBehaviour {
    private Vector3 targetPosition;

    private float movementSpeed = 5.0f;
    private float rotationSpeed = 2.0f;
    private float targetPositionTolerance = 3.0f;
    private float minX;
    private float maxX;
    private float minZ;
    private float maxZ;

    void Start() {
        minX = -45.0f;
        maxX = 45.0f;

        minZ = -45.0f;
        maxZ = 45.0f;

        //Get Wander Position
        GetNextPosition();
    }

    void Update() {
        if (Vector3.Distance(targetPosition, transform.position) <=
targetPositionTolerance) {
            GetNextPosition();
        }

        Quaternion targetRotation = Quaternion.LookRotation(targetPosition
```

```
    - transform.position);
            transform.rotation = Quaternion.Slerp(transform.rotation,
    targetRotation, rotationSpeed * Time.deltaTime);

            transform.Translate(new Vector3(0, 0, movementSpeed *
    Time.deltaTime));
        }

        void GetNextPosition() {
            targetPosition = new Vector3(Random.Range(minX, maxX), 0.5f,
    Random.Range(minZ, maxZ));
        }
    }
```

The `Wander` script generates a new random position in a specified range whenever the AI character reaches its current destination point. The `Update` method will then rotate our enemy and move it toward this new destination. Attach this script to our AI character so that it can move around in the scene. The `Wander` script is rather simplistic, but we will cover more advanced locomotion approaches in later chapters.

Using the Sense class

The `Sense` class is the interface of our sensory system that the other custom senses can implement. It defines two virtual methods, `Initialize` and `UpdateSense`, which will be implemented in custom senses, and are executed from the `Start` and `Update` methods, respectively.

 Virtual methods are methods that can be overridden using the `override` modifier in derived classes. Unlike `abstract` classes, virtual classes do not require that you override them.

The code in the `Sense.cs` file looks like this:

```
using UnityEngine;

public class Sense : MonoBehaviour {
    public bool enableDebug = true;
    public Aspect.AspectTypes aspectName = Aspect.AspectTypes.ENEMY;
    public float detectionRate = 1.0f;

    protected float elapsedTime = 0.0f;
```

```
protected virtual void Initialize() { }
protected virtual void UpdateSense() { }

// Use this for initialization
void Start ()
   {
   elapsedTime = 0.0f;
   Initialize();
}
// Update is called once per frame
void Update ()
   {
   UpdateSense();
}
}
```

The basic properties include its detection rate to execute the sensing operation, as well as the name of the aspect it should look for. This script will not be attached to any of our objects since we'll be deriving from it for our actual senses.

Giving a little perspective

The perspective sense will detect whether a specific aspect is within its field of view and visible distance. If it sees anything, it will take the specified action, which in this case is to print a message to the console.

The code in the `Perspective.cs` file looks like this:

```
using UnityEngine;

public class Perspective : Sense
{
    public int fieldOfView = 45;
    public int viewDistance = 100;

    private Transform playerTransform;
    private Vector3 rayDirection;

    protected override void Initialize()
    {
        playerTransform =
GameObject.FindGameObjectWithTag("Player").transform;
    }

    protected override void UpdateSense()
```

```
        {
            elapsedTime += Time.deltaTime;

            if (elapsedTime >= detectionRate)
            {
                DetectAspect();
            }
    }

    //Detect perspective field of view for the AI Character
    void DetectAspect()
    {
        RaycastHit hit;
        rayDirection = playerTransform.position - transform.position;

        if ((Vector3.Angle(rayDirection, transform.forward)) < fieldOfView)
        {
            // Detect if player is within the field of view
            if (Physics.Raycast(transform.position, rayDirection, out hit,
viewDistance))
            {
                Aspect aspect = hit.collider.GetComponent<Aspect>();
                if (aspect != null)
                {
                    //Check the aspect
                    if (aspect.aspectType != aspectName)
                    {
                        print("Enemy Detected");
                    }
                }
            }
        }
    }
```

We need to implement the `Initialize` and `UpdateSense` methods that will be called from the `Start` and `Update` methods of the parent `Sense` class, respectively. In the `DetectAspect` method, we first check the angle between the player and the AI's current direction. If it's in the field of view range, we shoot a ray in the direction that the player tank is located. The ray length is the value of the visible distance property.

The `Raycast` method will return when it first hits another object. This way, even if the player is in the visible range, the AI character will not be able to see if it's hidden behind the wall. We then check for an `Aspect` component, and it will return true only if the object that was hit has an `Aspect` component and its `aspectType` is different from its own.

The `OnDrawGizmos` method draws lines based on the perspective field of view angle and viewing distance so that we can see the AI character's line of sight in the editor window during play testing. Attach this script to our AI character and be sure that the aspect type is set to `ENEMY`.

This method can be illustrated as follows:

```
void OnDrawGizmos()
    {
        if (playerTransform == null)
        {
            return;
        }

        Debug.DrawLine(transform.position, playerTransform.position,
Color.red);

        Vector3 frontRayPoint = transform.position + (transform.forward *
viewDistance);

        //Approximate perspective visualization
        Vector3 leftRayPoint = frontRayPoint;
        leftRayPoint.x += fieldOfView * 0.5f;

        Vector3 rightRayPoint = frontRayPoint;
        rightRayPoint.x -= fieldOfView * 0.5f;

        Debug.DrawLine(transform.position, frontRayPoint, Color.green);
        Debug.DrawLine(transform.position, leftRayPoint, Color.green);
        Debug.DrawLine(transform.position, rightRayPoint, Color.green);
    }
}
```

Touching is believing

The next sense we'll be implementing is `Touch.cs`, which triggers when the player tank entity is within a certain area near the AI entity. Our AI character has a box collider component and its `IsTrigger` flag is on.

We need to implement the `OnTriggerEnter` event, which will be called whenever another collider enters the collision area of this game object's collider. Since our tank entity also has a collider and rigid body components, collision events will be raised as soon as the colliders of the AI character and player tank collide.

Unity provides two other trigger events besides `OnTriggerEnter`:
`OnTriggerExit` and `OnTriggerStay`. Use these to detect when a collider
leaves a trigger, and to fire off every frame that a collider is inside the
trigger, respectively.

The code in the `Touch.cs` file is as follows:

```
using UnityEngine;

public class Touch : Sense
{
    void OnTriggerEnter(Collider other)
    {
        Aspect aspect = other.GetComponent<Aspect>();
        if (aspect != null)
        {
            //Check the aspect
            if (aspect.aspectType != aspectName)
            {
                print("Enemy Touch Detected");
            }
        }
    }
}
```

Our sample NPC and tank have `BoxCollider` components on them already. The NPC has
its sensor collider set to `IsTrigger = true`. If you're setting up the scene on your own,
make sure you add the `BoxCollider` component yourself, and that it covers a wide enough
area to trigger easily for testing purposes. Our trigger can be seen in the following
screenshot:

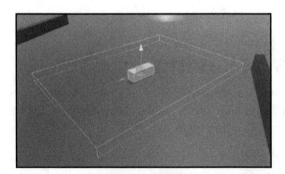

The collider around our player

The previous screenshot shows the box collider on our enemy AI that we'll use to trigger the touch sense event. In the following screenshot, we can see how our AI character is set up:

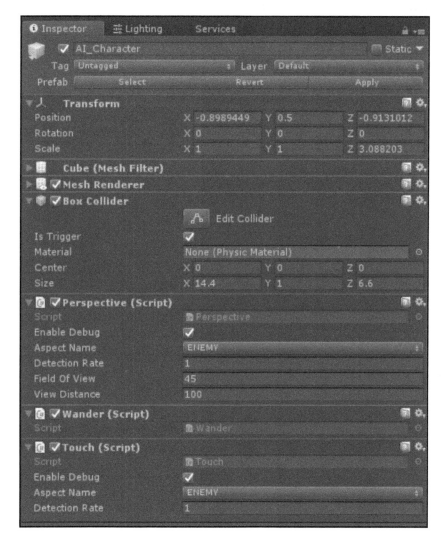

The properties of our NPC

For demo purposes, we just print out that the enemy aspect has been detected by the touch sense, but in your own games, you can implement any events and logic that you want. This system ties in really nicely with other concepts covered in this book, such as states, which we learned about in Chapter 2, *Finite State Machines and You*.

Testing the results

Hit play in the Unity editor and move the player tank near the wandering AI NPC by clicking on the ground to direct the tank to move to the clicked location. You should see the **Enemy touch detected** message in the console log window whenever our AI character gets close to our player tank:

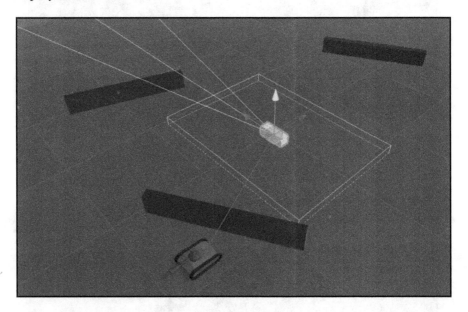

Our NPC and tank in action

The previous screenshot shows an AI agent with touch and perspective senses looking for another aspect. Move the player tank in front of the NPC, and you'll get the **Enemy detected** message. If you go to the editor view while running the game, you should see the debug lines being rendered. This is because of the OnDrawGizmos method implemented in the perspective Sense class.

Summary

This chapter introduced the concept of using sensors and implemented two distinct senses—perspective and touch—for our AI character. The sensory system is one component of the whole decision-making system. We can use the sensory system in combination with a behavior system to execute certain behaviors for certain senses. For example, we can use an FSM to change to **Chase** and **Attack** states from the **Patrol** state once we have detected that there's an enemy within line of sight. We'll also cover how to apply behavior tree systems in `Chapter 6`, *Behavior Trees*.

In the next chapter, we'll be looking at popular pathfinding algorithms. We'll learn how to make our AI agent navigate complex environments using the ever-popular A* pathfinding algorithm, and even Unity's own `NavMesh` system.

4
Finding Your Way

Obstacle avoidance is a simple behavior that allows AI entities to reach a target point. It's important to note that the specific behavior implemented in this chapter is meant to be used for behaviors such as crowd simulation, where the main objective of each agent entity is just to avoid the other agents and reach the target. There's no consideration of what would be the most efficient and shortest path. We'll learn about the A* Pathfinding algorithm in the next section.

In this chapter, we will cover the following topics:

- Path following and steering
- A custom A* Pathfinding implementation
- Unity's built-in NavMesh

Technical Requirements

You will be required to have Unity 2017 installed on a system that has either Windows 7 SP1+, 8, 10, 64-bit versions or Mac OS X 10.9+. The code in this book will not run on Windows XP and Vista, and server versions of Windows and OS X are not tested.

The code files of this chapter can be found on GitHub:
`https://github.com/PacktPublishing/Unity-2017-Game-AI-Programming-Third-Edition/tree/master/Chapter04`

Check out the following video to see the code in action:
`https://goo.gl/Eoxby1`

Following a path

Before diving into A*, which is a procedural approach to pathfinding, we'll implement a more rudimentary waypoint-based system. While more advanced techniques, such as the aforementioned A* method or Unity's NavMesh, will often be the preferred method for pathfinding, looking at a simpler, more pure version will help set the foundation for understanding more complex pathfinding approaches. Not only that, but there are many scenarios in which a waypoint-based system will be more than enough, and will allow more fine-tuned control over your AI agent's behavior.

In this example, we'll create a path, which is made up of individual waypoints. For our purposes, a waypoint is simply a point in space with an X, Y, and Z value; we can simply use a `Vector3` to represent this data. By making a serialized array of `Vector3` in our script, we'll be able to edit the points in the inspector without much fuss. If you want to challenge yourself and tweak this system to be a bit more user-friendly, you may want to consider using an array of game objects instead, and using their position (a `Vector3`) instead. For demonstration purposes, the example provided will stick to the `Vector3` array. After setting up some points in our array, we want to end up with a path that looks like the following screenshot:

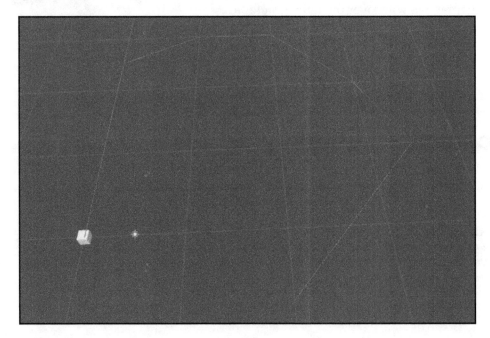

An object path

In the preceding screenshot, we use some debug lines to draw the connections between waypoints. Don't worry, there isn't any magic happening here. By using Unity's debug features, we can visualize the path we'll be having our agent traverse. Let's deconstruct our `Path.cs` script to see how we achieve this.

The path script

Here is our `Path.cs` script, which is responsible for managing our waypoints:

```
using UnityEngine;

public class Path: MonoBehaviour
{
    [SerializeField]
    private Vector3[] waypoints;

    public bool isDebug = true;
    public float radius = 2.0f;

    public float PathLength {
        get { return waypoints.Length; }
    }
    public Vector3 GetPoint(int index)
    {
        return waypoints[index];
    }
    private void OnDrawGizmos()
    {
        if (!isDebug) {
            return;
        }

        for (int i = 0; i < waypoints.Length; i++)
        {
            if (i + 1 < waypoints.Length)
            {
                Debug.DrawLine(waypoints[i], waypoints[i + 1], Color.red);
            }
        }
    }
}
```

The `SerializeField` property can be used to force Unity to serialize a private field, and display it in the inspector.

Our waypoints' `Vector3` array is the collection of waypoints in the path mentioned earlier. To initialize the waypoints, we must add the script to a game object in our scene. In the sample scene, we simply create an empty game object and attach the `Path.cs` script to it. For the sake of clarity, we've also renamed our game object to `Path`. With the `Path` game object ready to go, we can assign the path values in the inspector. The sample values look like this:

Path values provided in the sample project

The values in the screenshot here are arbitrary, and can be tweaked to your liking. You just need to make sure you have at least two waypoints along your path.

The `PathLength` property simply returns the length of our waypoint array. It provides a public getter for our private field, and is later used by another script. The `radius` variable allows us to define the tolerance for our pathfinding. Rather than expecting our agent to be at the precise location of our waypoint, we'll use a radius to determine when the agent is *close enough* to consider the waypoint visited. The `GetPoint` method is a simple helper to get a waypoint from the array at a given index.

It is common and proper practice to make fields `private` by default, especially when the data contained is integral to the functionality of the class. In our case, the waypoint order, array size, and more should not be modified at runtime, so we ensure that external classes can only get data from them by using helper methods and properties, and protect them from external changes by making them private.

Finally, we use `OnDrawGizmos`, which is a `MonoBehaviour` method that Unity automatically calls for us, to draw debug information in the scene view in the editor. We can toggle this functionality on and off by setting the value of `isDebug` to `true` or `false`, respectively.

Using the path follower

Next, we'll set up our agent to follow the path defined in the previous section. We'll use a simple cube in the example, but feel free to use any art you want. Let's take a closer look at the `Pathing.cs` script provided in the sample code:

```
public class Pathing : MonoBehaviour
{
    [SerializeField]
    private Path path;
    [SerializeField]
    private float speed = 20.0f;
    [SerializeField]
    private float mass = 5.0f;
    [SerializeField]
    private bool isLooping = true;
    private float currentSpeed;
    private int currentPathIndex = 0;
    private Vector3 targetPoint;
    private Vector3 direction;
    private Vector3 targetDirection;
```

The first group of fields are variables we want serialized so that they can be set via the inspector. path is a reference to the Path object we created earlier; we can simply drag and drop the component from the path game object into this field. speed and mass are used to calculate the movement of the agent along the path. isLooping is used to determine whether or not we should loop around the path. When true, the agent will reach the last waypoint, then go to the first waypoint on the path and start over. Once the values are all assigned, the inspector should look something like this:

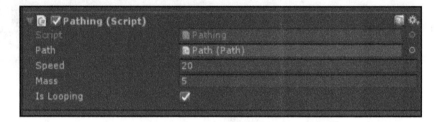

The pathfinding script inspector with its default values

Our Start method handles the initialization for some of the remaining private fields—direction and targetPoint:

```
private void Start ()
    {
        // Initialize the direction as the agent's current facing direction
        direction = transform.forward;
        // We get the firt point along the path
        targetPoint = path.GetPoint(currentPathIndex);
    }
```

Our Update method does a few things for us. First, it does some boilerplate null safety checks, it updates the speed of the agent, checks whether the target has been reached, calls the SetNextTarget method to determine the next target point, and finally, applies the direction and rotation changes as needed:

```
private void Update ()
    {
        if(path == null) {
            return;
        }

        currentSpeed = speed * Time.deltaTime;
        if(TargetReached())
        {
            if (!SetNextTarget()) {
```

```
        return;
      }
    }

    direction += Steer(targetPoint);
    transform.position += direction; //Move the agent according to the
direction
    transform.rotation = Quaternion.LookRotation(direction); //Rotate
the agent towards the desired direction
  }
```

To keep things nice and readable, we moved some of the functionality out of the Update method. TargetReached is fairly straightforward. It uses the radius of path to determine if the agent is *close enough* to the target waypoint, as you can see here:

```
private bool TargetReached()
{
    return (Vector3.Distance(transform.position, targetPoint) <
path.radius);
}
```

The SetNextTarget method is a bit more interesting. As you can see, it returns a bool. If we haven't reached the end of the array, it'll just increment the value, but if the method is unable to set the next point, because we've reached the end of the array, and isLooping is false, it returns false. If you go back to our Update method for a moment, you'll see that when this happens, we simply return out of Update and do nothing. This is because we've reached the end of the road, and there is nowhere else for our agent to go. In the same scenario, but with isLooping == true evaluating to true, we reset our next target point to the first in the array (0):

```
private bool SetNextTarget()
{
    bool success = false;
    if (currentPathIndex < path.PathLength - 1) {
        currentPathIndex++;
        success = true;
    }
    else
    {
        if(isLooping)
        {
            currentPathIndex = 0;
            success = true;
        }
        else
        {
```

```
                    success = false;
            }
        }
        targetPoint = path.GetPoint(currentPathIndex);
        return success;
    }
```

The `Steer` method uses the given target point and does some calculations to get the new direction and rotation. By subtracting the target point (*b*) from the current position (*a*), we get a vector for the direction from *a* to *b*. We normalize that vector, then apply the current speed to determine how far to move this frame along the new `targetDirection`. Lastly, we use the mass to ease the acceleration between our `targetDirection` and our current direction, and return that value as `acceleration`:

```
public Vector3 Steer(Vector3 target)
{
    // Subtracting vector b - a gives you the direction from a to b.
    targetDirection = (target - transform.position);
    targetDirection.Normalize();
    targetDirection*= currentSpeed;
    Vector3 steeringForce = targetDirection - direction;
    Vector3 acceleration = steeringForce / mass;
    return acceleration;
}
```

When you run the scene, the agent cube will follow the path as expected. If you toggle `isLooping` off, the agent will reach the final waypoint and stop there, but if you leave it on, the agent will loop around the path infinitely. Try tweaking the various settings to see how it affects the outcome.

Avoiding obstacles

Next, we'll look at an obstacle avoidance mechanic. To get started, pop open the same scene, named `ObstacleAvoidance`. The sample scene is quite straightforward. Aside from the camera and directional light, there is a plane with a series of blocks that will act as our obstacles, a cube that will act as our agent, and a canvas containing some instructional text. The scene will look like the following screenshot:

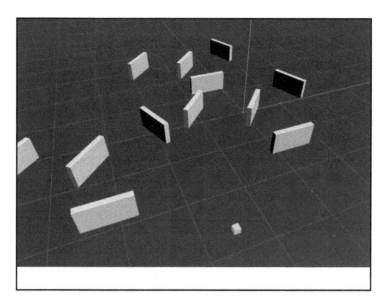

The sample scene setup

The hierarchy for the preceding scene pictures looks like this:

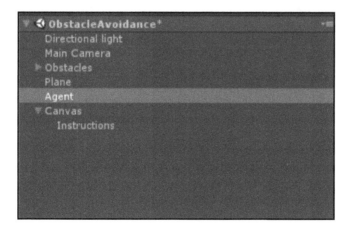

The organized hierarchy

It is worth noting that this `Agent` object is not a pathfinder. As such, if we set too many walls up, our `Agent` might have a hard time finding the target. Try a few wall setups and see how our `Agent` performs.

Adding a custom layer

Our mechanic relies on raycasting to detect obstacles. Rather than just assuming every single object is an obstacle, we specifically use a layer named **Obstacles** and filter out everything else. This is not a default layer in Unity, so we have to set it up manually. The sample project already has this set up for you, but if you wanted to add your own layer, you could access the layer setup window in two different ways. The first is through the menus—**Edit | Project Settings | Tags and Layers**—and the second method is by selecting the layer dropdown in the hierarchy and selecting **Add Layer....**The following screenshot shows the menu's location in the upper-right corner of the inspector:

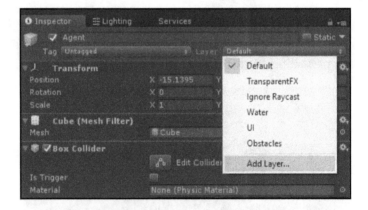

Selecting the **Tags and Layers** menu through the menu shown in the preceding screenshot, or through Unity's menu bar, will open up a window where you can freely add, edit, or remove layers (and tags, but we're not interested in those at the moment). Let's add `Obstacles` in the 8th slot, as shown in this screenshot:

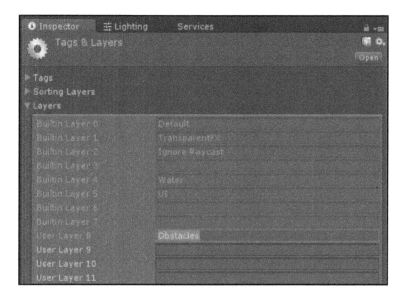

Creating a new layer

You should save the project after you make any changes to the settings, but there is no dedicated save button for layers specifically. You can now assign the layer in the same dropdown in the inspector as the one we just used, as depicted in the following screenshot:

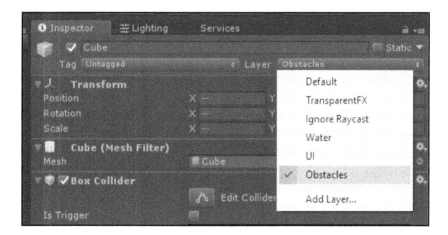

Assigning our new layer

Layers are most commonly used by cameras to render a part of the scene, and by lights to illuminate only some parts of the scene. But they can also be used by raycasting to selectively ignore colliders or create collisions. You can learn more about this at http://docs.unity3d.com/Documentation/Components/Layers.html.

Obstacle avoidance

Now that our scene is set up, let's take a look at our avoidance behavior script. It contains all the logic for driving our agent, and applies the avoidance to the movement of the agent. In the sample project, take a look at the Avoidance.cs script:

```
using UnityEngine;

public class Avoidance : MonoBehaviour
{
    [SerializeField]
    private float movementSpeed = 20.0f;
    [SerializeField]
    private float rotationSpeed = 5.0f;
    [SerializeField]
    private float force = 50.0f;
    [SerializeField]
    private float minimumAvoidanceDistance = 20.0f;
    [SerializeField]
    private float toleranceRadius = 3.0f;
    private float currentSpeed;
    private Vector3 targetPoint;
    private RaycastHit mouseHit;
    private Camera mainCamera;
    private Vector3 direction;
    private Quaternion targetRotation;
    private RaycastHit avoidanceHit;
    private Vector3 hitNormal;
    private void Start ()
    {
        mainCamera = Camera.main;
        targetPoint = Vector3.zero;
    }
```

You'll find some familiar field names in the preceding code snippet. Values such as movement speed, rotation speed, tolerance radius, and more are similar to values we used in our waypoint system. Similarly, we use the `SerializeField` attribute to expose our private fields in the inspector for easy editing and assignment, while protecting our values from being tampered with by external objects at runtime. In the `Start` method, we simply initialize some values. For example, we cache a reference to our `Camera.main` here so that we don't have to do the lookup every single time we need a reference to it. Next, let's look at the `Update` method:

```
private void Update ()
{
        CheckInput();
        direction = (targetPoint - transform.position);
        direction.Normalize();

        //Apply obstacle avoidance
        ApplyAvoidance(ref direction);

        //Don't move the agent when the target point is reached
        if(Vector3.Distance(targetPoint, transform.position) <
toleranceRadius) {
             return;
        }
        currentSpeed = movementSpeed * Time.deltaTime;

        //Rotate the agent towards its target direction
        targetRotation = Quaternion.LookRotation(direction);
        transform.rotation = Quaternion.Slerp(transform.rotation,
targetRotation, rotationSpeed *                    Time.deltaTime);

        //Move the agent forard
        transform.position += transform.forward * currentSpeed;
    }
```

Right off the bat, we call `CheckInput()`, which looks like this:

```
private void CheckInput()
{
    if (Input.GetMouseButtonDown(0))
    {
        var ray = mainCamera.ScreenPointToRay(Input.mousePosition);
        if (Physics.Raycast(ray, out mouseHit, 100.0f)) {
            targetPoint = mouseHit.point;
        }
    }
}
```

We check whether the user has clicked the left mouse button (by default, it is the button mapped to "0"). If so, we check for a physics raycast originating from the main camera, shooting to the position of the mouse. If we get a positive hit, we simply assign the hit point from `mouseHit` to be our new `targetPoint`. This is where our agent will attempt to move to. Back to `Update`, we have the following lines, right after our `CheckInput()` method:

```
direction = (targetPoint - transform.position);
direction.Normalize();

//Apply obstacle avoidance
ApplyAvoidance(ref direction);
```

We calculate the direction to our target point, in the same way we did in our `Pathing.cs` script, and we normalize that vector so that it has a magnitude of no more than 1. Next, we modify that direction and apply avoidance, by sending that direction vector to our `ApplyAvoidance()` method, which looks like this:

```
private void ApplyAvoidance(ref Vector3 direction)
{
    //Only detect layer 8 (Obstacles)
    //We use bitshifting to create a layermask with a value of
    //0100000000 where only the 8th position is 1, so only it is active.
    int layerMask = 1 << 8;

    //Check that the agent hit with the obstacles within it's minimum
distance to avoid
    if (Physics.Raycast(transform.position, transform.forward, out
avoidanceHit, minimumAvoidanceDistance, layerMask))
    {
        //Get the normal of the hit point to calculate the new direction
        hitNormal = avoidanceHit.normal;
        hitNormal.y = 0.0f; //Don't want to move in Y-Space

        //Get the new directional vector by adding force to agent's current
forward vector
        direction = transform.forward + hitNormal * force;
    }
}
```

Before digging into the preceding code, it's important to understand how Unity handles masking layers. As we mentioned earlier, we want our raycast to only hit the layers we care about, in this case, our `Obstacles` layer. If you were observant, you might have noticed our layer's array has 32 slots, from index 0 to 31. We put our `Obstacles` layer on slot 8 (index 9). The reason for this is that Unity represents the layers using a 32-bit int, and each bit represents one of the slots, from right to left. Let's break that down visually.

Let's say we want to represent a layer mask, where only the first slot (the first bit) is active. In this case, we'd assign the bit a value of 1. It would look like this:

```
0000 0000 0000 0000 0000 0000 0000 0001
```

And if you're still solid on your computer science fundamentals, you'll remember, that in binary, that value translates to an int value of 1. Let's say you have a mask that only has the first four slots/indices selected. That would like like this:

```
0000 0000 0000 0000 0000 0000 0000 1111
```

Once again, converting from binary, it gives us an int value of *15 (1 + 2+ 4 + 8)*.

In our script, we want a mask with only the 9th position active, which would look like this:

```
0000 0000 0000 0000 0000 0001 0000 0000
```

Again, doing the math, we know that the int value for that mask is 256. But doing the math manually is inconvenient. Luckily, C# provides some operators to manipulate bits. This line in the preceding code does just that:

```
int layerMask = 1 << 8;
```

It uses a bit shift operator—the left-shift operator, specifically—to create our mask. The way it works is fairly straightforward: it takes an int operand (the int value on the left-hand side of the expression) with a value of 1, then shifts that bit representation to the left eight times. It looks something like this:

```
0000 0000 0000 0000 0000 0000 0000 0001 //Int value of 1
                              <<<< <<<< //Shift left 8 times
0000 0000 0000 0000 0000 0001 0000 0000 //Int value of 256
```

As you can see, bitwise operators are helpful, and though they don't always lead to very readable code, they're very handy in situations like this one.

 You can also find a good discussion on using layermasks on Unity3D online. The question-and-answer site can be found at http://answers.unity3d.com/questions/8715/how-do-i-use-layerma sks.html. Alternatively, you may consider using LayerMask.GetMask(), which is Unity's built-in method for dealing with named layers.

With that out of the way, let's go back to the rest of our `ApplyAvoidance()` code. After creating the layer mask, the following lines look like this:

```
//Check that the agent hit with the obstacles within it's minimum distance
to avoid
if (Physics.Raycast(transform.position, transform.forward, out
avoidanceHit, minimumAvoidanceDistance,      layerMask))
{
    //Get the normal of the hit point to calculate the new direction
    hitNormal = avoidanceHit.normal;
    hitNormal.y = 0.0f; //Don't want to move in Y-Space

    //Get the new direction vector by adding force to agent's current
forward vector
    direction = transform.forward + hitNormal * force;
}
```

Once again, we use a raycast, but this time, the origin is the position of the agent, and the direction is its forward vector. You'll also notice that we use an overload of the `Physics.Raycast()` method that takes our `layerMask` as an argument, meaning our raycast will only hit objects in our obstacles layer. When a hit does occur, we get the normal of the surface we hit and calculate the new direction vector.

The last bit of our `Update` function looks like this:

```
//Don't move the agent when the target point is reached
if(Vector3.Distance(targetPoint, transform.position) < toleranceRadius) {
    return;
}
currentSpeed = movementSpeed * Time.deltaTime;

//Rotate the agent towards its target direction
targetRotation = Quaternion.LookRotation(direction);
transform.rotation = Quaternion.Slerp(transform.rotation, targetRotation,
rotationSpeed *                 Time.deltaTime);

//Move the agent forard
transform.position += transform.forward * currentSpeed;
```

Again, you may recognize some of this code, as it's very similar to the code used in the `Pathing.cs` script. If we've come within the acceptable radius of our destination, we do nothing. Otherwise, we rotate the agent and move it forward.

In the sample scene, you can find an `Agent` game object with the `Avoidance.cs` script attached. The inspector with all the values assigned will look like this:

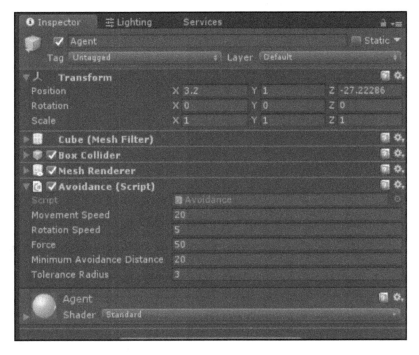

Agent inspector view

Try tweaking the values to see what kinds of results you can get. Simply hit play and click around the scene to tell your agent to move. You may notice that, even though the agent is intelligently avoiding the obstacles, it won't always take the most efficient route to its target destination. That's where A* comes in.

A* Pathfinding

Next up, we'll implement the A* algorithm in a Unity environment using C#. The A* Pathfinding algorithm is widely used in games and interactive applications even though there are other algorithms, such as Dijkstra's algorithm, because of its simplicity and effectiveness. We've briefly covered this algorithm previously, in `Chapter 1`, *The Basics of AI in Games*, but let's review the algorithm again from an implementation perspective.

Revisiting the A* algorithm

We briefly touched on the A* algorithm earlier in the book, so let's review the basics before we dive into our implementation. For starters, we need to create a grid-based representation of our map. The best option for this is a 2D array. This grid and all of its associated data will be contained in our `GridManager` class. The `GridManager` class will contain a list of `Node` objects that represent each cell in our grid. The nodes themselves will contain some additional data about themselves, such as their heuristic cost and whether or not they are an obstacle node.

We'll also need to keep two lists—our open list, that is, our list of nodes to explore, and our closed list, which will contain nodes we've already visited. We'll implement these in our `PriorityQueue` class, which provides some additional helper functionality.

In essence, our A* algorithm, implemented in the `AStar` class, must do the following:

1. Begin at the starting node and put it in the open list.
2. As long as the open list has some nodes in it, we'll perform the following processes:
    1. Pick the first node from the open list and keep it as the current node. (This is assuming that we've sorted the open list and the first node has the least cost value, which will be mentioned at the end of the code.)
    2. Get the neighboring nodes of this current node that are not obstacle types, such as a wall or canyon, that can't be passed through.
    3. For each neighbor node, check if this neighbor node is already in the closed list. If not, we'll calculate the total cost (F) for this neighbor node using the following formula:

        ```
        F = G + H
        ```

    4. In the preceding formula, G is the total cost from the start node to this node and H is the total cost from this node to the final target node.
    5. Store this cost data in the neighbor node object. Also, store the current node as the parent node as well. Later, we'll use this parent node data to trace back the actual path.
    6. Put this neighbor node in the open list. Sort the open list in ascending order, ordered by the total cost to reach the target node.
    7. If there are no more neighbor nodes to process, put the current node in the closed list and remove it from the open list.
    8. Go back to step 2 using the next node in the open list.

Once you have completed this process, your current node should be in the target goal node position, but only if there's an obstacle-free path to reach the goal node from the start node. If it is not at the goal node, there's no available path to the target node from the current node position. If there's a valid path, all we have to do now is trace back from the current node's parent node until we reach the start node again. This will give us a path list of all the nodes that we chose during our pathfinding process, ordered from the target node to the start node. We then just reverse this path list, since we want to know the path from the start node to the target goal node.

This is a general overview of the algorithm we're going to implement in Unity using C#. So, let's get started.

Implementation

In order to get started with A*, we'll have to take the concepts and apply them as concrete implementations in the code. In our sample code, we break the A* system into a few key components: the `Node`, `GridManager`, `PriorityQueue`, and `AStart` classes.

Let's break down what each class does in the following few sections.

The Node class

We can think of the `Node` class as a container for all of the relevant information about each tile in our grid. We store information about things such as the cost of the node, the parent of the node, and its position:

```
using UnityEngine;
using System;

public class Node : IComparable
{
    //Total cost so far for the node
    public float gCost;
    //Estimated cost from this node to the goal node
    public float hCost;
    //Is this an obstacle node
    public bool bObstacle;
    //Parent of the node in the linked list
    public Node parent;
    //Position of the node in world space
    public Vector3 position;
    public Node()
```

```
    {
        hCost = 0.0f;
        gCost = 1.0f;
        bObstacle = false;
        parent = null;
    }
    public Node(Vector3 pos)
    {
        hCost = 0.0f;
        gCost = 1.0f;
        bObstacle = false;
        parent = null;

        position = pos;
    }
    public void MarkAsObstacle()
    {
        bObstacle = true;
    }
    //IComparable Interface method implementation
    public int CompareTo(object obj)
    {
        Node node = (Node)obj;
        if (hCost < node.hCost)
        {
            return -1;
        }
        if (hCost > node.hCost)
        {
            return 1;
        }
        return 0;
    }
}
```

In code, we represent our G and H costs as `gCost` and `hCost`, respectively. G refers to the cost from the start node to this node, and H refers to the estimated cost from this node to the end node. Depending on how comfortable you get with A*, you might consider renaming them something a bit more descriptive. In our example, we want to adhere as closely as possible to the *on paper* version of the names of concepts, for the purpose of explaining the C# implementation.

The class provides a simple constructor that takes no arguments, and one overload that takes in a position, which prepopulates the position field with the passed-in value. There's nothing too fancy here.

You may have noticed that our class implements the IComparable interface, which requires us to implement the CompareTo() method to satisfy the interface contract requirements.

 You can think of an interface as a contract. On its own, it does nothing. You cannot implement any logic in an interface. By inheriting from an interface, you're simply agreeing to implement all the methods with the provided signatures in the implementing class. That way, any other class that wants to call a given method from an interface on your class can assume that the method exists.

The actual implementation of the method compares the given node to this node based on their hCost. We'll take a look at its usage later on.

Establishing the priority queue

We represent our open and closed list using the PriorityQueue class. This approach allows us to implement some helper methods for our own convenience. The PriorityClass.cs file looks like this:

```
using System.Collections;

public class PriorityQueue
{
    private ArrayList nodes = new ArrayList();
    public int Length
    {
        get { return nodes.Count; }
    }
    public bool Contains(object node)
    {
        return nodes.Contains(node);
    }
    public Node GetFirstNode()
    {
        if (nodes.Count > 0)
        {
            return (Node)nodes[0];
        }
        return null;
    }
    public void Push(Node node)
    {
        nodes.Add(node);
```

```
        nodes.Sort();
    }

    public void Remove(Node node)
    {
        nodes.Remove(node);
        nodes.Sort();
    }
}
```

There isn't much of note in this code, but the `Sort()` method in particular is interesting. Remember the `CompareTo()` method in the `Node` class? The `ArrayList.Sort()` actually relies on the implementation of `CompareTo()` in the node class to sort the array. More specifically, it will sort according to the node's `hCost`.

Setting up our grid manager

The `GridManager` class does a lot of the heavy lifting in terms of arranging and visualizing our grid. Compared to some of the code we've seen so far in this book, it's a fairly lengthy class, since it provides several helper methods. Pop open the `GridManager.cs` class to follow along:

```
[SerializeField]
private int numberOfRows = 20;
[SerializeField]
public int numberOfColumns = 20;
[SerializeField]
public float gridCellSize = 2;
[SerializeField]
public bool showGrid = true;
[SerializeField]
public bool showObstacleBlocks = true;

private Vector3 origin = new Vector3();
private GameObject[] obstacleList;
private Node[,] nodes { get; set; }
```

We start off by setting up some variables. We specify how many rows and columns are in our grid, and we specify their size (in world units). There isn't much else of note here, but we should point out that the `Node[,]` syntax indicates that we are initializing a 2D array of `nodes`, which makes sense, since a grid is a 2D array itself.

In our `Awake` method, we see the following line:

```
obstacleList = GameObject.FindGameObjectsWithTag("Obstacle");
```

This simply initializes the `obstacleList` game object array by finding things tagged as
"Obstacle". `Awake` then calls two setup methods: `InitializeNodes()` and
`CalculateObstacles()`:

```
private void InitializeNodes()
{
    nodes = new Node[numberOfColumns, numberOfRows];

    int index = 0;
    for (int i = 0; i < numberOfColumns; i++)
    {
        for (int j = 0; j < numberOfRows; j++)
        {
            Vector3 cellPosition = GetGridCellCenter(index);
            Node node = new Node(cellPosition);
            nodes[i, j] = node;
            index++;
        }
    }
}
```

The names of these methods are to the point, so as you may have guessed,
`InitializeNodes()` initializes our nodes, and does so by populating the `nodes` 2D array.
This code invokes a helper method, `GetGridCellCenter()`, which we'll look at later on,
but the approach is fairly straightforward. We loop through the 2D array, column by
column and row by row, and we create nodes spaced apart according to the grid size:

```
private void CalculateObstacles()
{
    if (obstacleList != null && obstacleList.Length > 0)
    {
        foreach (GameObject data in obstacleList)
        {
            int indexCell = GetGridIndex(data.transform.position);
            int column = GetColumnOfIndex(indexCell);
            int row = GetRowOfIndex(indexCell);
            nodes[row, column].MarkAsObstacle();
        }
    }
}
```

The `CalculateObstacles()` method simply runs through the list of obstacles we initialized during `Awake`, determines which grid slot the obstacle occupies, and marks the node at that grid slot as an obstacle using `MarkAsObtacle()`.

The `GridManager` class has a few helper methods to traverse the grid and get the grid cell data. The following is a list of some of them with brief descriptions of what they do. The implementation is simple, so we won't go into the details:

- `GetGridCellCenter`: Given an index for a cell, it returns the center position (in world space) of that cell.
- `GetGridCellPositionAtIndex`: Returns the origin position of the cell (the corner). Used as a helper for `GetGridCellCenter`.
- `GetGridIndex`: Given a position (as a `Vector3` in world space), it returns the cell closest to the position.
- `GetRowOfIndex` and `GetColumnOfIndex`: Just as the names say, they return the row or column of the cell at the given index. For example, in a 2 x 2 grid, the cell at index 2 (starting from 0), would be in row 2, column 1.

Next, we have some methods that help with figuring out the neighbors to a given node:

```
public void GetNeighbors(Node node, ArrayList neighbors)
{
    Vector3 neighborPosition = node.position;
    int neighborIndex = GetGridIndex(neighborPosition);

    int row = GetRowOfIndex(neighborIndex);
    int column = GetColumnOfIndex(neighborIndex);

    //Bottom
    int leftNodeRow = row - 1;
    int leftNodeColumn = column;
    AssignNeighbor(leftNodeRow, leftNodeColumn, neighbors);

    //Top
    leftNodeRow = row + 1;
    leftNodeColumn = column;
    AssignNeighbor(leftNodeRow, leftNodeColumn, neighbors);

    //Right
    leftNodeRow = row;
    leftNodeColumn = column + 1;
    AssignNeighbor(leftNodeRow, leftNodeColumn, neighbors);

    //Left
```

```
        leftNodeRow = row;
        leftNodeColumn = column - 1;
        AssignNeighbor(leftNodeRow, leftNodeColumn, neighbors);
    }
    // Check the neighbor. If it's not an obstacle, assign the neighbor.
    private void AssignNeighbor(int row, int column, ArrayList neighbors)
    {
        if (row != -1 && column != -1 && row < numberOfRows && column <
numberOfColumns)
        {
            Node nodeToAdd = nodes[row, column];
            if (!nodeToAdd.bObstacle)
            {
                neighbors.Add(nodeToAdd);
            }
        }
    }
}
```

First, we have `GetNeighbors()`, which uses the given node's position in the grid to figure out which cells are to the bottom, top, right, and left of it. It assigns the node as a neighbor using `AssignNeighbor()`, which does some validation, such as checking that the potential neighbor is within bounds (of the array), and that the neighbor is not marked as an obstacle.

Lastly, we have `OnDrawGizmos()` and `DebugDrawGrid()`, which display the grid of the size we specified in our scene view for debugging. Next up, the meat and potatoes. We tie it all together with our `AStar` class.

Diving into our A* implementation

The `AStar` class is the actual implementation of the A* algorithm. This is where the magic happens. The code in the `AStar.cs` file looks like this:

```
using UnityEngine;
using System.Collections;

public class AStar
{
    public static PriorityQueue closedList;
    public static PriorityQueue openList;
    private static ArrayList CalculatePath(Node node)
    {
        ArrayList list = new ArrayList();
        while (node != null)
        {
            list.Add(node);
```

```
            node = node.parent;
        }
        list.Reverse();
        return list;
    }


    /// Calculate the estimated Heuristic cost to the goal
    private static float EstimateHeuristicCost(Node curNode, Node goalNode)
    {
        Vector3 vecCost = curNode.position - goalNode.position;
        return vecCost.magnitude;
    }
    // Find the path between start node and goal node using A* Algorithm
    public static ArrayList FindPath(Node start, Node goal)
    {
        openList = new PriorityQueue();
        openList.Push(start);
        start.gCost = 0.0f;
        start.hCost = EstimateHeuristicCost(start, goal);

        closedList = new PriorityQueue();
        Node node = null;
        GridManager gridManager =
GameObject.FindObjectOfType<GridManager>();
        if(gridManager == null) {
            return null;
        }

        while (openList.Length != 0)
        {
            node = openList.GetFirstNode();

            if (node.position == goal.position)
            {
                return CalculatePath(node);
            }
            ArrayList neighbors = new ArrayList();
            gridManager.GetNeighbors(node, neighbors);
            //Update the costs of each neighbor node.
            for (int i = 0; i < neighbors.Count; i++)
            {
                Node neighborNode = (Node)neighbors[i];

                if (!closedList.Contains(neighborNode))
                {
                  //Cost from current node to this neighbor node
                  float cost = EstimateHeuristicCost(node, neighborNode);
                  //Total Cost So Far from start to this neighbor node
```

```
                    float totalCost = node.gCost + cost;
                    //Estimated cost for neighbor node to the goal
                    float neighborNodeEstCost =
    EstimateHeuristicCost(neighborNode, goal);
                    //Assign neighbor node properties
                    neighborNode.gCost = totalCost;
                    neighborNode.parent = node;
                    neighborNode.hCost = totalCost + neighborNodeEstCost;
                    //Add the neighbor node to the open list if we haven't
    already done so.
                    if (!openList.Contains(neighborNode))
                    {
                        openList.Push(neighborNode);
                    }
                }
            }
            closedList.Push(node);
            openList.Remove(node);
        }

        //We handle the scenario where no goal was found after looping
    thorugh the open list
        if (node.position != goal.position)
        {
            Debug.LogError("Goal Not Found");
            return null;
        }

        //Calculate the path based on the final node
        return CalculatePath(node);
    }
}
```

There is quite a bit to go over here, so let's break it down, step by step:

```
    public static PriorityQueue closedList;
    public static PriorityQueue openList;
```

We start off by declaring our open and closed lists, which will contain visited and non-visited nodes, respectively:

```
    private static float EstimateHeuristicCost(Node currentNode, Node goalNode)
    {
        Vector3 cost= currentNode.position - goalNode.position;
        return cost.magnitude;
    }
```

In the preceding code, we implement a method called `EstimateHeuristicCost` to calculate the cost between the two given nodes. The calculation is simple. We just find the direction vector between the two by subtracting one position vector from another. The magnitude of this resultant vector gives the direct distance from the current node to the goal node.

Next, we have our `FindPath` method, which does most of the work:

```
public static ArrayList FindPath(Node start, Node goal)
{
    openList = new PriorityQueue();
    openList.Push(start);
    start.gCost = 0.0f;
    start.hCost = EstimateHeuristicCost(start, goal);

    closedList = new PriorityQueue();
    Node node = null;

    GridManager gridManager = GameObject.FindObjectOfType<GridManager>();
    if(gridManager == null) {
        return null;
    }
```

It initializes our open and closed lists. At first, we'll only have the starting node in our `openList`. We also initialize the `gCost`, which is zero, because the distance to the starting node (itself) is zero. We then assign the `hCost` using the `EstimateHeuristicCost()` method we just discussed.

We'll need a reference to our `GridManager` going forward, so we get it using `FindObjectOfType()` and do some null checking. Next, we begin processing the open list:

```
while (openList.Length != 0)
{
    node = openList.GetFirstNode();

    if (node.position == goal.position)
    {
        return CalculatePath(node);
    }
    ArrayList neighbors = new ArrayList();
    gridManager.GetNeighbors(node, neighbors);
    //Update the costs of each neighbor node.
    for (int i = 0; i < neighbors.Count; i++)
    {
        Node neighborNode = (Node)neighbors[i];
```

```
            if (!closedList.Contains(neighborNode))
            {
                //Cost from current node to this neighbor node
                float cost = EstimateHeuristicCost(node, neighborNode);
                //Total Cost So Far from start to this neighbor node
                float totalCost = node.gCost + cost;
                //Estimated cost for neighbor node to the goal
                float neighborNodeEstCost =
EstimateHeuristicCost(neighborNode, goal);
                //Assign neighbor node properties
                neighborNode.gCost = totalCost;
                neighborNode.parent = node;
                neighborNode.hCost = totalCost + neighborNodeEstCost;
                //Add the neighbor node to the open list if we haven't
already done so.
                if (!openList.Contains(neighborNode))
                {
                    openList.Push(neighborNode);
                }
            }
        }
        closedList.Push(node);
        openList.Remove(node);
    }

    //We handle the scenario where no goal was found after looping thorugh
the open list
    if (node.position != goal.position)
    {
        Debug.LogError("Goal Not Found");
        return null;
    }

    //Calculate the path based on the final node
    return CalculatePath(node);
}
```

This code implementation resembles the A* algorithm that we have previously discussed. This would be a good time to brush up on it.

In plain English, the preceding code can be described as following these steps:

1. Get the first node of our `openList`. Keep in mind that our `openList` is always sorted after a new node is added so that the first node is always the node with the lowest estimated cost to the goal node.
2. Check whether the current node is already at the goal node. If so, exit the `while` loop and build the `path` array.
3. Create an array list to store the neighboring nodes of the current node being processed. Use the `GetNeighbors()` method to retrieve the neighbors from the grid.
4. For every node in the `neighbors` array, we check whether it's already in the `closedList`. If not, we calculate the cost values, update the node properties with the new cost values as well as the parent node data, and put it in `openList`.
5. Push the current node to `closedList` and remove it from `openList`. Rinse and repeat.

If there are no more nodes in the `openList`, our current node should be at the target node if there's a valid path available. Then, we just call the `CalculatePath()` method with the current node as the argument. The `CalcualtePath()` method looks like this:

```
private static ArrayList CalculatePath(Node node)
{
    ArrayList list = new ArrayList();
    while (node != null)
    {
      list.Add(node);
      node = node.parent;
    }
    list.Reverse();
    return list;
}
```

The `CalculatePath` method traces through each node's parent node object and builds an array list. This gives us an array list with nodes from the target node to the start node. Since we want a path array from the start node to the target node, we just call the `Reverse` method. And that's it! With our algorithm and helper classes out of the way, we can move on to our test script, which ties it all together.

Implementing a TestCode class

Now that we have the A* algorithm implemented via our `AStar` class (and the associated helper classes), we actually implement it using the `TestCode` class. The `TestCode.cs` file looks like this:

```
using UnityEngine;
using System.Collections;

public class TestCode : MonoBehaviour
{
    private Transform startPosition;
    private Transform endPosition;

    public Node startNode { get; set; }
    public Node goalNode { get; set; }

    private ArrayList pathArray;

    private GameObject startCube;
    private GameObject endCube;
    private float elapsedTime = 0.0f;
    public float intervalTime = 1.0f;
    private GridManager gridManager;
```

We declare our variables here, and once again set up a variable to hold a reference to our `GridManager`. Then, the `Start` method does some initialization and fires off our `FindPath()` method, as shown in this code:

```
    private void Start ()
    {
        gridManager = FindObjectOfType<GridManager>();
        startCube = GameObject.FindGameObjectWithTag("Start");
        endCube = GameObject.FindGameObjectWithTag("End");

        //Calculate the path using our AStart code.
        pathArray = new ArrayList();
        FindPath();
    }
    private void Update ()
    {
        elapsedTime += Time.deltaTime;
```

```
        if(elapsedTime >= intervalTime)
        {
            elapsedTime = 0.0f;
            FindPath();
        }
    }
```

In the `Update` method, we check for the path at intervals, which is a brute force approach to refreshing the path if the goal moves at runtime. You may want to consider implementing this code using an event to avoid unnecessary overhead in every frame (or interval, in this case). The `FindPath()` method called in `Start` looks like this:

```
private void FindPath()
{
    startPosition = startCube.transform;
    endPosition = endCube.transform;
    startNode = new
Node(gridManager.GetGridCellCenter(gridManager.GetGridIndex(startPosition.p
osition)));
    goalNode = new
Node(gridManager.GetGridCellCenter(gridManager.GetGridIndex(endPosition.pos
ition)));

    pathArray = AStar.FindPath(startNode, goalNode);
}
```

First, it takes the positions of our start and end game objects. Then, it creates new `Node` objects using the helper methods `GridManager` and `GetGridIndex` to calculate their respective row and column index positions inside the grid. With those necessary values ready to go, we just call the `AStar.FindPath` method with the start node and goal node, and store the returned array list in the local `pathArray` variable.

Next, we implement the `OnDrawGizmos` method to draw and visualize the path found:

```
private void OnDrawGizmos()
{
    if (pathArray == null)
    {
        return;
    }

    if (pathArray.Count > 0)
    {
        int index = 1;
        foreach (Node node in pathArray)
        {
```

```
            if (index < pathArray.Count)
            {
                Node nextNode = (Node)pathArray[index];
                Debug.DrawLine(node.position, nextNode.position,
    Color.green);
                index++;
            }
        };
    }
}
```

We look through our `pathArray` and use the `Debug.DrawLine` method to draw the lines connecting the nodes from the `pathArray`. With this, we'll be able to see a green line connecting the nodes from start to end, forming a path, when we run and test our game.

Testing it in the sample scene

The sample scene looks like this:

Our sample scene with the pathfinding grid drawn over it

As you can see in the preceding screenshot, there is a red starting node, a green goal node, a plane, and some light grey obstacles.

The following screenshot is a snapshot of our scene hierarchy:

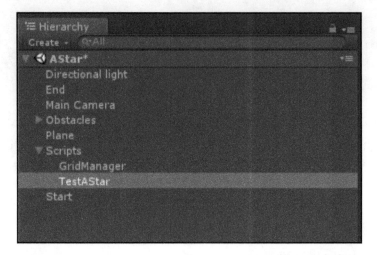

There are a few things to note in the preceding screenshot (and yes, you can ignore the **Directional light**, as it's just here to make our scene look pretty). First, we have grouped all of our obstacles under a parent Obstacles transform. Second, we have separate game objects for our TestCode class and our GridManager class as children under the Scripts game object. As you saw in the code sample earlier, there are some fields exposed in the GridManager, which should look like the following screenshot in our sample scene:

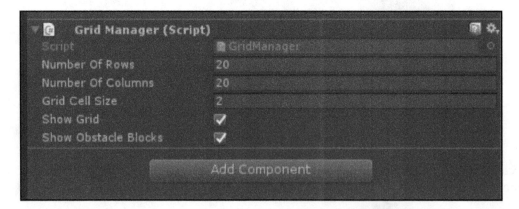

As you can see in the previous screenshot, we have **Show Grid** ticked to true. This will enable us to see the grid in the scene view.

Testing all the components

Now that we've looked at how everything is wired up, hit the play button and observe how a path will be drawn from our start node to our goal node, as shown in the following screenshot:

Since we're checking for the path at intervals inside the `Update` loop, we can move the goal node in play mode, and see the path updated. The following screenshot shows the new path after moving our goal node to a different location:

As you can see, since the goal is closer, so is the most optimal path to reach it. In a little more than a nutshell, that is A*. A very powerful algorithm can be distilled down to a few classes totaling a few hundred lines of code (with most of it due to formatting and commenting).

A* vs IDA*

In Chapter 1, *The Basics of AI in Games*, we mentioned some of the differences between A* and IDA*. Now that you've implemented A*, you can see that the A* implementation keeps a few things in memory—the path array, the open list, and the closed list. At different points in the implementation, you may allocate more or less memory as you iterate through your lists. In this regard, A* is greedier than IDA*, but keep in mind that in most cases, on modern hardware, this is not an issue—even with much larger grids than ours.

The IDA* approach only looks at the the current iteration's adjacent/neighbor spots, and because it keeps no record of the visited nodes, it may end up visiting the same node multiple times. In similar circumstances, this means a much lower memory overhead than the faster A* version.

While the point can be argued, it is this humble author's opinion that IDA* is not a relevant pattern in modern game development—even on resource-conscious applications, such as mobile games. In other fields, one could make a stronger case for the iterative deepening approach, but, fortunately, even aging mobile devices have copious amounts of memory relative to the needs of the 99% of games that will implement some sort of pathfinding.

Navigation mesh

Next, we'll learn how to use Unity's built-in navigation mesh generator that can make pathfinding for AI agents a lot easier. Early in the Unity 5.x cycle, NavMesh was made available to all users, including personal edition licensees, whereas it was previously a Unity Pro-only feature. Before the release of 2017.1, the system was upgraded to allow a component-based workflow, but as it requires an additional downloadable package that, at the time of writing is only available as a preview, we will stick to the default scene-based workflow. Don't worry, the concepts carry over, and when the final implementation eventually makes its way to 2017.x, there shouldn't be drastic changes.

> For more information on Unity's NavMesh component system, head over to GitHub: https://github.com/Unity-Technologies/NavMeshComponents.

Now, we will dive in and explore all that this system has to offer. AI pathfinding needs a representation of the scene in a particular format; we've seen that using a 2D grid (array) for A* Pathfinding on a 2D map. AI agents need to know where the obstacles are, especially the static obstacles. Dealing with collision avoidance between dynamically moving objects is another subject, primarily known as steering behaviors. Unity has a built-in tool for generating a NavMesh that represents the scene in a context that makes sense for our AI agents to find the optimum path to the target. Pop open the demo project and navigate to the NavMesh scene to get started.

Inspecting our map

Once you have the demo scene, NavMesh, open, it should look something like this screenshot:

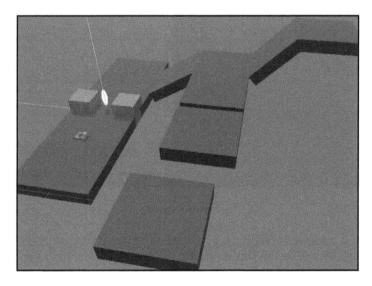

A scene with obstacles and slopes

This will be our sandbox to explain and test the NavMesh system functionality. The general setup is similar to an RTS (real-time strategy) game. You control the blue tank. Simply click at a location to make the tank move to that location. The yellow indicator is the current target location for the tank.

Navigation Static

The first thing to point out is that you need to mark any geometry in the scene that will be baked into the NavMesh as **Navigation Static**. You may have encountered this elsewhere, such as in Unity's light-mapping system, for example. Setting game objects as static is easy. You can easily toggle the Static flag on for all purposes (navigation, lighting, culling, batching and so on), or you can use the dropdown to specifically select what you want. The toggle is found in the top-right corner of the inspector for the selected object(s). Look at this screenshot for a general idea of what you're looking for:

The Navigation Static property

You can do this on a per-object basis, or, if you have a nested hierarchy of game objects in your hierarchy, you can apply the setting to the parent and Unity will prompt you to apply it to all children.

Baking the navigation mesh

The navigation settings for the navigation mesh are applied via the **Navigation** window on a scene-wide basis. You can open the window by navigating to **Window** | **Navigation** in the menu bar. Like any other window, you can detach it to be free-floating, or you can dock it. Our screenshots show it docked as a tab next to the hierarchy, but you can place this window anywhere you please.

With the window open, you'll notice four separate tabs. It'll look something like this screenshot:

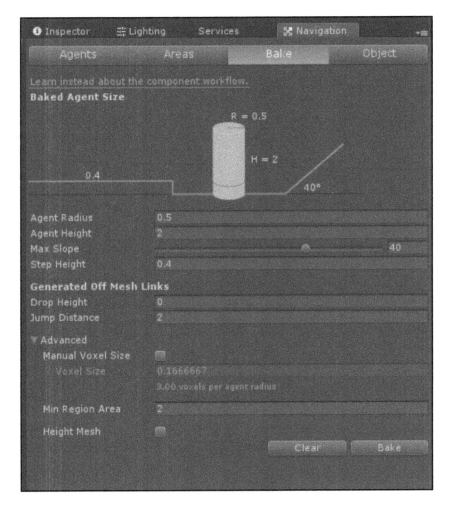

The Navigation window

In our case, the preceding screenshot shows the **Bake** tab selected, but your editor might have one of the other tabs selected by default.

Let's take a look at each tab, starting from the left and working our way to the right, starting with the **Agents** tab, which looks like the following screenshot:

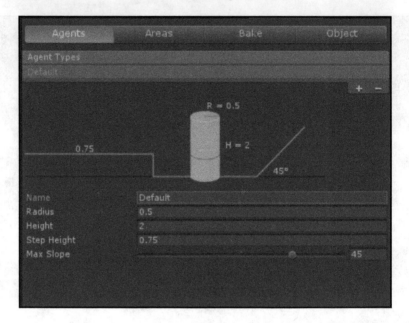

The Agents tab

If you're working on a different project, you may find that some of these settings are different than what we set them to in the sample project from which the preceding screenshot was taken. At the top of the tab, you can see a list where you can add additional agent types by pressing the "+" button. You can remove any of these additional agents by selecting it and pressing the "-" button. The window provides a nice visual of what the various settings do as you tweak them. Let's take a look at what each setting does:

- **Name**: The name of the agent type to be displayed in the **Agent Types** dropdown.
- **Radius**: Think of it as the agent's "personal space". Agents will try to avoid getting too cozy with other agents based on this value, as it uses it for avoidance.
- **Height**: As you may have guessed, it dictates the height of the agent, which it can use for vertical avoidance (passing under things, for example).
- **Step Height**: This value determines how high of an obstacle the agent can climb over.

- **Max Slope**: As we'll see in the coming section, this value determines the max angle up which an agent can climb. This can be used to make steep areas of the map inaccessible to the agent.

Next, we have the **Areas** tab, which looks like the following screenshot:

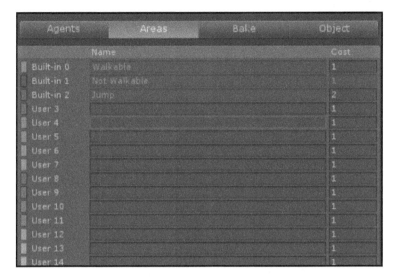

As you can see in the preceding screenshot, Unity provides some default area types that cannot be edited: **Walkable**, **Not Walkable**, and **Jump**. In addition to naming and creating new areas, you can assign default costs to these areas.

Areas serve two purposes: making areas accessible or inaccessible per agent, and marking areas as less desirable in terms of navigation cost. For example, you may have an RPG where demon enemies cannot enter areas marked as "holy ground." You could also have areas of your map marked something like "marsh" or "swamp," which your agent could avoid based on the cost.

The third tab, **Bake**, is probably the most important. It allows you to create the actual NavMesh for your scene. You'll recognize some of the settings. The **Bake** tab looks like this:

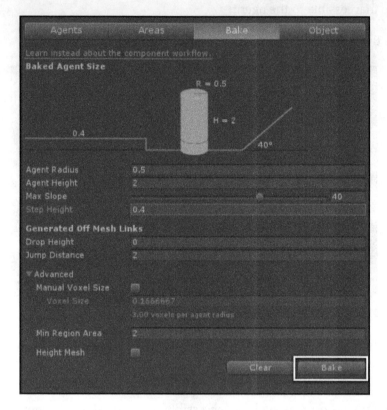

The Bake tab

The agent size settings in this tab dictate how agents interact with the environment, whereas the settings in the **Agents** tab dictate how they interact with other agents and moving objects, but they control the same parameters, so we'll skip those here. The **Drop Height** and **Jump Distance** control how far an agent can "jump" to reach a portion of the NavMesh that is not directly connected to the one the agent is currently on. We'll go over this in more detail up ahead, so don't sweat it if you're not quite sure what that means yet.

There are also some advanced settings that are generally collapsed by default. Simply click the drop-down triangle by the **Advanced** heading to unfold these options. You can think of the **Manual Voxel Size** setting as the "quality" setting. The smaller the size, the more detail you can capture in the mesh. The **Min Region Area** is used to skip baking platforms or surfaces below the given threshold. The **Height Mesh** gives you more detailed vertical data when baking the mesh. For example, it will help preserve the proper placement of your agent when climbing up stairs.

The **Clear** button will clear any NavMesh data for the scene, and the **Bake** button will create the mesh for your scene. The process is fairly fast. As long as you have the window selected, you'll be able to see the NavMesh generated by the **Bake** button in your scene view. Go ahead and hit the **Bake** button to see the results. In our sample scene, you should end up with something that looks like the following screenshot:

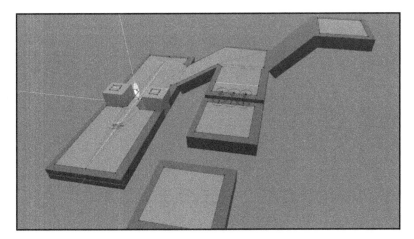

The blue areas represent the NavMesh. We'll revisit this up ahead. For now, let's move on to the final tab, the **Object** tab, which looks like the following screenshot:

The three buttons pictured in the preceding screenshot, **All**, **Mesh Renderers**, and **Terrains**, act as filters for your scene. These are helpful when working in complex scenes with lots of objects in the hierarchy. Selecting an option will filter out that type in your hierarchy to make them easier to select. You can use this when digging through your scene looking for objects to mark as navigation static.

Using the NavMesh agent

Now that we have our scene set up with a NavMesh, we need a way for our agent to use this information. Luckily for us, Unity provides a **Nav Mesh Agent** component we can throw onto our character. The sample scene has a game object named `Tank` with the component already attached to it. Take a look at it in the hierarchy, and it should look like the following screenshot:

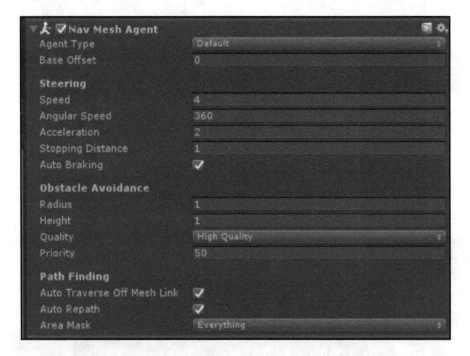

There are quite a few settings here, and we won't go over all of them, since they're fairly self-explanatory and you can find the full descriptions in the official Unity documentation, but let's point out a few key things:

- **Agent Type**: Remember the **Agents** tab in the **Navigation** window? The agent types you define there will be selectable here.

- **Auto Traverse Off Mesh Link**: We'll get into Off Mesh Links up ahead, but this setting allows the agent to automatically use that feature.
- **Area Mask**: The areas you set up in the **Areas** tab of the **Navigation** window will be selectable here.

That's it. The component handles 90% of the heavy lifting for you: placement on the path, pathfinding, obstacle avoidance, and so on. The only thing you need to do is provide the agent with a target destination. Let's look at that next.

Setting a destination

Now that we've set up our AI agent, we need a way to tell it where to go. Our sample project provides a script named `Target.cs` that does just that.

This is a simple class that does three things:

- Shoots a ray from the camera origin to the mouse world position using a ray
- Updates the marker position
- Updates the destination property of all the NavMesh agents

The code is fairly straightforward. The entire class looks like this:

```
using UnityEngine;
using UnityEngine.AI;

public class Target : MonoBehaviour
{
    private NavMeshAgent[] navAgents;
    public Transform targetMarker;

    private void Start ()
    {
      navAgents = FindObjectsOfType(typeof(NavMeshAgent)) as
NavMeshAgent[];
    }

    private void UpdateTargets ( Vector3 targetPosition )
    {
      foreach(NavMeshAgent agent in navAgents)
      {
        agent.destination = targetPosition;
      }
    }
}
```

```
    private void Update ()
    {
        if(GetInput())
        {
            Ray ray = Camera.main.ScreenPointToRay(Input.mousePosition);
            RaycastHit hitInfo;

            if (Physics.Raycast(ray.origin, ray.direction, out hitInfo))
            {
                Vector3 targetPosition = hitInfo.point;
                UpdateTargets(targetPosition);
                targetMarker.position = targetPosition;
            }
        }
    }

    private bool GetInput()
    {
        if (Input.GetMouseButtonDown(0))
        {
            return true;
        }
        return false;
    }

    private void OnDrawGizmos()
    {
        Debug.DrawLine(targetMarker.position, targetMarker.position +
Vector3.up * 5, Color.red);
    }
}
```

There are a few things happening here. In the `Start` method, we initialize our `navAgents` array by using the `FindObjectsOfType()` method.

The `UpdateTargets()` method runs through our `navAgents` array and sets their target destination to the given `Vector3`. This is really the key to making it work. You can use any mechanism you wish to actually get the target destination, and all you need to do to get the agent to move there is set the `NavMeshAgent.destination` field; the agent will do the rest.

Our sample uses a click-to-move approach, so whenever the player clicks, we shoot a ray from the camera into the world towards the mouse cursor, and if we hit something, we assign that hit position as the new `targetPosition` for the agent. We also set the target marker accordingly for easy in-game visualization of the target destination.

To test it out, make sure you baked the NavMesh as described in the previous section, then enter play mode, and select any area on the map. If you go click-happy, you may notice there are some areas your agent *can't* reach—the top of the red cubes, the top-most platform, and the platform towards the bottom of the screen.

In the case of the red cubes, they're too far up. The ramp leading up to the top-most platform is too steep, as per our **Max Slope** settings, and the agent can't climb up to it. The following screenshots illustrate how the **Max Slope** settings affect the NavMesh:

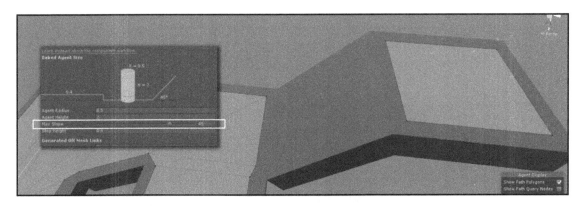

NavMesh with the max slope value set to 45

If you tweak the **Max Slope** to something like **51**, then hit the **Bake** button again to re-bake the NavMesh, it will yield results like this:

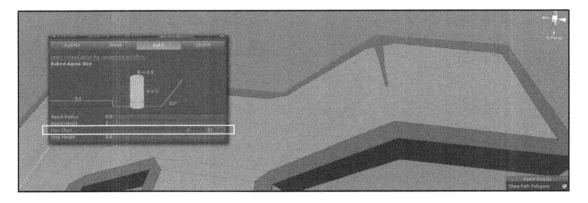

NavMesh with the max slope value set to 51

As you can see, you can tweak your level design to make entire areas inaccessible by foot with a simple value tweak. An example where this would be helpful is if you had a platform or ledge that you need a rope, ladder, or elevator to get to. Maybe even a special skill, such as the ability to climb? I'll let your imagination do the work and think of all the fun ways to use this.

Making sense of Off Mesh Links

You may have noticed that our scene features two gaps. The first one is accessible to our agent, but the one near the bottom of the screen is too far away. This is not completely arbitrary. Unity's **Off Mesh Links** effectively bridge the gap between segments of the NavMesh that are not connected. You can see these links in the editor, as shown in the next screenshot:

The blue circles with the connecting lines are links

There are two ways that Unity can generate these links. The first we've already covered. Remember the **Jump Distance** value in the **Bake** tab of the **Navigation** window? Unity will automatically use that value to generate the links for us when baking the NavMesh. Try tweaking the value in our test scene to 5 and re-baking. Notice how, now, the platforms are linked? That's because the meshes are within the newly-specified threshold.

Set the value back to 2 and re-bake. Now, let's look at the second method. Create spheres that will be used to connect the two platforms. Place them roughly as shown in the following screenshot:

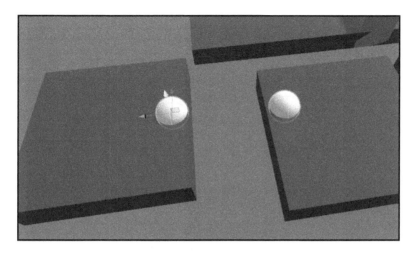

You may already see where this is going, but let's walk through the process to get these connected. In this case, I've named the sphere on the right start, and the sphere on the left end. You'll see why in a second. Next up, add the **Off Mesh Link** component on the platform on the right (relative to the preceding screenshot). You'll notice the component has start and end fields. As you may have guessed, we're going to drop the spheres we created earlier into their respective slots—the start sphere in the start field, and the end sphere in the end field. Our inspector will look something like this:

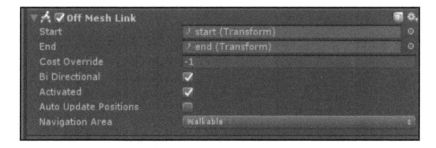

The **Cost Override** value kicks in when you set it to a positive number. It will apply a cost multiplier to using this link, as opposed to, potentially, a more cost-effective route to the target.

The **Bi Directional** value allows the agent to move in both directions when set to true. You can turn this off to create one-way links in your level design. The **Activated** value is just what it says. When set to false, the agent will ignore this link. You can turn it on and off to create gameplay scenarios where the player has to hit a switch to activate it, for example.

You don't have to re-bake to enable this link. Take a look at your NavMesh and you'll see that it looks like the following screenshot:

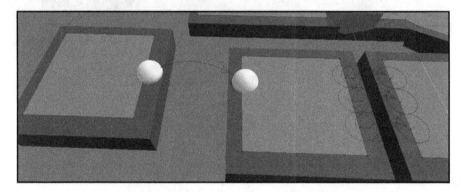

As you can see, the smaller gap is still automatically connected, and now we have a new link generated by our **Off Mesh Link** component between the two spheres. Enter play mode and click on the far platform, and, as expected, the agent can now navigate to the detached platform, as you can see in the following screenshot:

In your own levels, you may need to tweak these settings to get the exact results you expect, but combining these features gives you a lot of power out-of-the-box. You can have a simple game up and running fairly quickly using Unity's NavMesh feature.

Summary

You have now navigated your way to the end of this chapter (pun unapologetically intended). From simple waypoints, to the efficient and fast A* algorithm, to Unity's own powerful and robust NavMesh system, we've added some important and flexible tools to your game-making toolbelt. Not only do these concepts play well with each other, but they also work well with other systems we've already seen in this book, and we'll explore in those next few chapters.

In the next chapter, we'll start to look at how we can create efficient and realistic simulations for groups of agents that need to move in unison. Let's get to it!

5

Flocks and Crowds

Flocks and crowds are two additional core AI concepts we'll be exploring in this book. As you'll see in this chapter, flocks are relatively simple to implement, and they add a fairly extraordinary amount of realism to your simulation in just a few lines of code. Crowds can be a bit more complex, but we'll be exploring some of the powerful tools that come bundled with Unity to get the job done. In this chapter, we'll cover the following topics:

- Learning the history of flocks and herds
- Understanding the concepts behind flocks
- Flocking using the traditional algorithm
- Using realistic crowds

Technical Requirements

You will be required to have Unity 2017 installed on a system that has either Windows 7 SP1+, 8, 10, 64-bit versions or Mac OS X 10.9+. The code in this book will not run on Windows XP and Vista, and server versions of Windows and OS X are not tested.

The code files of this chapter can be found on GitHub:
`https://github.com/PacktPublishing/Unity-2017-Game-AI-Programming-Third-Edition/tree/master/Chapter05`

Check out the following video to see the code in action:
`https://goo.gl/SHdto4`

Learning the origins of flocks

The flocking algorithm dates all the way back to the mid-80s. It was first developed by *Craig Reynolds*, who developed it for use in films, the most famous adaptation of the technology being the swarm of bats in *Batman Returns* in 1992, for which he won an Oscar. Since then, the use of the flocking algorithm has expanded beyond the world of film into various fields, from games to scientific research. Despite being relatively efficient and accurate, the algorithm is also very simple to understand and implement.

Understanding the concepts behind flocks and crowds

As with previous concepts, it's easiest to understand flocks and herds by relating them to the real-life behaviors they model. As simple as it sounds, these concepts describe a group of objects, or boids as they are called in artificial intelligence lingo, moving together as a group. The flocking algorithm gets its name from the behavior birds exhibit in nature, where a group of birds follow one another toward a common destination, mostly keeping a fixed distance from each other. The emphasis here is on the group. We've explored how single agents can move and make decisions on their own, but flocks are a relatively computationally efficient way of simulating large groups of agents moving in unison while modeling unique movement in each boid that doesn't rely on randomness or predefined paths.

The implementation that we'll be building in this chapter for flocking is built upon the concepts originally developed by Craig Reynolds himself. There are many ways to approach Reynolds' flocking behavior, and in our example we've gone with a single-threaded optimized version that allocates no memory. Performance will vary based on the hardware, but generally speaking, the more boids in your flock, the more CPU time it will take to compute the swarm's direction. There are three basic concepts that define how a flock works, and these concepts have been around since the algorithm's introduction in the 80s:

- **Separation**: This means maintaining a distance with other neighbors in the flock to avoid collision. The following diagram illustrates this concept:

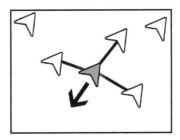

Diagram of separation in flocking

In the preceding image, the middle boid is shown moving in a direction away from the rest of the boids, without changing its heading.

- **Alignment**: This means to moving in the same direction as the flock, and with the same velocity. The following image illustrates this concept:

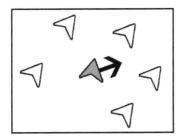

Diagram of alignment in flocking

In the preceding image, the boid in the middle is shown changing its heading toward the arrow to match the heading of the boids surrounding it.

- **Cohesion**: This means maintaining a maximum distance from the flock's center. The following image illustrates this concept:

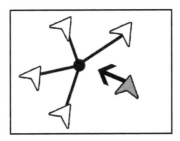

Diagram of cohesion in flocking

In the preceding image, the boid to the right of the flock moves in the direction of the arrow to be within the minimum distance to its nearest group of boids.

Using the Reynolds algorithm

Without further ado, let's dive into the Reynolds flocking algorithm. There are two main scripts for our flocking implementation: `Boid.cs` and `FlockController.cs`. The sample code for this chapter provides a scene with all the necessary setup for testing. You'll also notice a third script named `TargetMovement.cs`, which we use to move a target that our flock will follow around the scene.

For our boid, we can use a simple cube as a prefab. Of course, feel free to replace the cube with any art you want. Let's add the `Boid.cs` script to our boid prefab. The code looks like this:

```
using UnityEngine;

public class Boid : MonoBehaviour
{
    [SerializeField]
    private FlockController flockController;
    //The modified direction for the boid.
    private Vector3 targetDirection;
    //The Boid's current direction.
    private Vector3 direction;

    public FlockController FlockController
    {
        get { return flockController; }
        set { flockController = value; }
    }
    public Vector3 Direction { get { return direction; }}

    private void Awake()
    {
        direction = transform.forward.normalized;
        if(flockController != null)
        {
            Debug.LogError("You must assign a flock controller!");
        }
    }

    private void Update() {
        targetDirection = FlockController.Flock(this,
```

```
transform.localPosition, direction);
        if(targetDirection == Vector3.zero)
        {
            return;
        }
        direction = targetDirection.normalized;
        direction *= flockController.SpeedModifier;
        transform.Translate(direction * Time.deltaTime);
    }
}
```

Right off the bat, you'll notice a reference to `FlockController`, which we will create next. You can think of `FlockController` as the shared brain of the swarm/flock. Each boid does not need to be aware of its neighbors directly, because `FlockController` handles this information separately. This allows us to keep the boid code nice and tidy.

We initialize the direction vector in our `Awake` method, and we make sure that the `FlockController` is assigned, or we log an error. There are several ways you can enforce null-safety, such as creating the instance if not provided, but in our case we'll assume you assigned the value via the inspector.

The `Update` method does the rest of the workit calls the `Flock()` method on `FlockController` and passes in a reference to itself, its local position, and its direction. This will return a vector that we then normalize to keep movement from appearing jerky or too fast, and apply the movement by using `Transform.Translate()`. As usual, make sure you're easing the movement over the `Time.deltaTime` to ensure smooth frame-to-frame movement.

It's important to note that we make sure to cache as many `Vector3` variables as needed. Avoid allocations by avoiding the use of `new Vector3()` where possible.

Implementing the FlockController

The `FlockController` is going to handle the orchestration of the entire flock. There is a quite a bit going on here in terms of variables. Let's take a look at `FlockController.cs` chunk by chunk:

```
private int flockSize = 20;
```

Here, we simply assign the size of our flock. You'll see this value being used up ahead in the `Awake` method:

```
private float speedModifier = 5;

[SerializeField]
private float alignmentWeight = 1;

[SerializeField]
private float cohesionWeight = 1;

[SerializeField]
private float separationWeight = 1;

[SerializeField]
private float followWeight = 5;
```

We then declare a series of modifier and weight values. `speedModifier` directly affects how fast our boids can move. Tweak this as needed. The three values following `speedModifier` are weight values for alignment, cohesion, and separation, respectively. These values will multiply their weight in the final calculation of all the direction vectors that drive the movement of the boid. `followWeight` is used to weight the effect of the target's delta versus the boid. If you want the boids to follow the target more closely, increase this value.

```
[SerializeField]
private Boid prefab;
[SerializeField]
private float spawnRadius = 3.0f;
private Vector3 spawnLocation = Vector3.zero;

[SerializeField]
public Transform target;
```

The following chunk of variables defines some more setup variables that we assign in the inspector. First, we have the prefab of the boid to spawn (which should have the `Boid.cs` component attached to it). `spawnRadius` is used to avoid artifacts that may come from spawning all the boids on top of each other if we were to spawn them all on one point. Instead, we spawn them within the given radius, as defined in this variable. Lastly, `target` is a reference to the transform of the target our flock/swarm will follow. In our test scene, it's a sphere with the `TargetMovement.cs` component attached to it.

Let's take a look at the `Awake` method:

```
private void Awake()
{
    flockList = new List<Boid>(flockSize);
    for (int i = 0; i < flockSize; i++)
    {
        spawnLocation = Random.insideUnitSphere * spawnRadius +
transform.position;
        Boid boid = Instantiate(prefab, spawnLocation, transform.rotation)
as Boid;

        boid.transform.parent = transform;
        boid.FlockController = this;
        flockList.Add(boid);
    }
}
```

We iterate through a loop enough times to spawn enough boids for our `flockSize`
variable. This is where our `spawnLocation` and `spawnRadius` come into play. Unity's
`Random.insideUnitSphere` generates the random position, which we add to our
transform's position to get the actual spawn location. We then instantiate the boid prefab,
while assigning to a `Boid` instance, which we then add to our `flockList`. Also note that
we assign the boid instance's `FlockController` property in this step.

Keep in mind that instantiating prefabs can be slow in Unity, so increasing the number of
boids in the flock will lead to a huge performance dip during the instantiation frame.

The only other method in this class is the `Flock()` method, which we saw being called
from `Boid` earlier. This does all the computation for the individual boids' directions. It looks
like this:

```
public Vector3 Flock(Boid boid, Vector3 boidPosition, Vector3
boidDirection)
{
    flockDirection = Vector3.zero;
    flockCenter = Vector3.zero;
    targetDirection = Vector3.zero;
    separation = Vector3.zero;

    for (int i = 0; i < flockList.Count; ++i)
    {
        Boid neighbor = flockList[i];
        //Check only against neighbors.
        if (neighbor != boid)
        {
```

```
                //Aggregate the direction of all the boids.
                flockDirection += neighbor.Direction;
                //Aggregate the position of all the boids.
                flockCenter += neighbor.transform.localPosition;
                //Aggregate the delta to all the boids.
                separation += neighbor.transform.localPosition - boidPosition;
                separation *= -1;
            }
        }
        //Alignment. The average direction of all boids.
        flockDirection /= flockSize;
        flockDirection = flockDirection.normalized * alignmentWeight;

        //Cohesion. The centroid of the flock.
        flockCenter /= flockSize;
        flockCenter = flockCenter.normalized * cohesionWeight;

        //Separation.
        separation /= flockSize;
        separation = separation.normalized * separationWeight;

        //Direction vector to the target of the flock.
        targetDirection = target.localPosition - boidPosition;
        targetDirection = targetDirection * followWeight;

        return flockDirection + flockCenter + separation + targetDirection;
    }
```

The method takes some information about our `Boid`, as well as a copy of it. We then iterate through every boid in the `flockList` and assign the boid at the current iteration's index to a temporary value called `neighbor`. To avoid doing multiple loops, we do several things in the same `for` loop:

- Sum up all the neighbors' directions
- Sum up all the neighbors' positions
- Sum up the position deltas to all neighbors

Once done with the loop (and thus aggregating all of the preceding values), we calculate the following:

- The flock direction, which we get by averaging the direction of all the boids. Since we've already got the sum of all the directions, we just divide it by the number of boids, the `flockSize`. We then normalize the value and apply the weight we defined earlier. This will give us our alignment.

- Similarly, we get the centroid of the flock by averaging all the positions of all the boids. As with direction, we normalize the vector before applying the weighting. The `flockCenter` gives us our cohesion vector.
- You may be seeing a pattern here, right? As with the previous two values, we average, normalize, then weight our separation value.
- `targetDirection` is a bit different. We first take the delta between the boid's position and the target's position, then we apply the weight. We don't normalize this value in this implementation, but feel free to experiment by doing so. Normalizing this value won't break the simulation, but you may notice your boids casually floating away from the target if it moves too fast.

With all of the values—cohesion, alignment, and separation—calculated, we add them up and return them to the `Boid` instance that called the method. The boid will use this vector as its target direction, as we saw in the `Boid.cs` file.

Because we could potentially have dozens or hundreds of boids, it's important to avoid any unnecessary computations at runtime. If you profile our implementation, you'll notice it allocates no memory whatsoever, meaning you won't have any annoying stuttering due to garbage collection. While the system will slow down as the boid count goes into the hundreds due to its single-threaded nature, having a few dozen boids is very fast. As you can see in the following screenshot, having a small flock flying around can be computed in less than a millisecond:

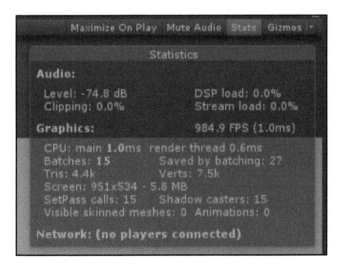

The stats panel showing our scene's performance

The flock target

Last, but not least, we have our flock target. To reiterate, you can use any art you like, or you can stick with the handsome little sphere in the provided sample project. The code for the target component is in the `TargetMovement.cs` file. The contents look like this:

```
using UnityEngine;

public class TargetMovement : MonoBehaviour
{
    [SerializeField]
    private Vector3 bounds;
    [SerializeField]
    private float moveSpeed = 10.0f;
    [SerializeField]
    private float turnSpeed = 3.0f;
    [SerializeField]
    private float targetPointTolerance = 5.0f;

    private Vector3 initialPosition;
    private Vector3 nextMovementPoint;
    private Vector3 targetPosition;
    private void Awake()
    {
        initialPosition = transform.position;
        CalculateNextMovementPoint();
    }

    private void Update ()
    {
        transform.Translate(Vector3.forward * moveSpeed * Time.deltaTime);
        transform.rotation = Quaternion.Slerp(transform.rotation,
Quaternion.LookRotation(nextMovementPoint - transform.position), turnSpeed
* Time.deltaTime);

        if(Vector3.Distance(nextMovementPoint, transform.position) <=
targetPointTolerance)
        {
            CalculateNextMovementPoint();
        }
    }

    private void CalculateNextMovementPoint()
    {
        float posX = Random.Range(initialPosition.x - bounds.x,
initialPosition.x + bounds.x);
        float posY = Random.Range(initialPosition.y - bounds.y,
```

```
initialPosition.y + bounds.y);
        float posZ = Random.Range(initialPosition.z - bounds.z,
initialPosition.z + bounds.z);
        targetPosition.x = posX;
        targetPosition.y = posY;
        targetPosition.z = posZ;
        nextMovementPoint = initialPosition + targetPosition;
    }
}
```

There are two main chunks of work in this class. First, Update moves the game object towards the forward vector, while rotating it towards the targetPosition. We provide two variables to modify the move and turn speed: moveSpeed and turnSpeed, respectively. We then check whether we've arrived at the destination point by comparing the distance to it against a tolerance radius that we define in targetPointTolerance. If we're close enough, we then set the next target point by calling CalculateNextMovementPoint().

In CalculateNextMovementPoint(), we set a random target position, but constrain it based on our bounds values, relative to the position of the target when we first run the script, as we set the initialPosition in Awake. Constraining this point will prevent the target from slowly deviating away from our game area and floating off into the sunset. Dramatic as it may be, it's not quite the effect we're going for here.

The scene layout

Now that we have all of our code covered, let's take a look at our scene. Our sample scene looks like the following screenshot:

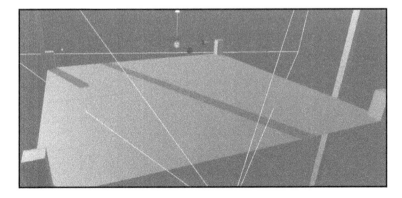

An overview of our scene layout

As you can see in the preceding screenshot, there isn't a lot of complexity to our setup. We have a plane, some environment cubes for perspective, a light, a camera, and our target. The full hierarchy looks like the following screenshot:

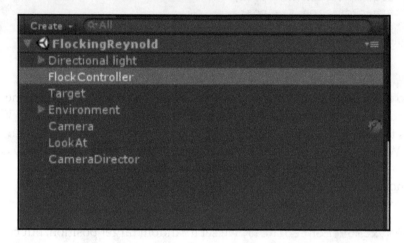

Our scene hierarchy with FlockController highlighted

As you can see from the preceding screenshot, we have a **Directional light**, and nested underneath it is a reflection probe. This is strictly for making the scene look nice, and has essentially no functional value, but hey, a little vanity never hurt anyone! We then have an empty game object named **FlockController**, which our FlockController script is attached to. The **Target** game object is a sphere with a bright yellow material and the TargetMovement script attached to it. All of the environment blocks are nested under the **Environment** game object, which in this case is a plane. The last three items are there to drive our camera, which will automatically lock on to our target, and keep it in frame. As it is outside the scope of this book, we'll skip over how the camera works, but if you're the curious type, you'll want to explore the official Unity documentation for more information on **Cinemachine** and **Timeline**, which drive the camera in our scene.

Back to the matter at hand—let's take a look at the `FlockController`, which looks like the following screenshot:

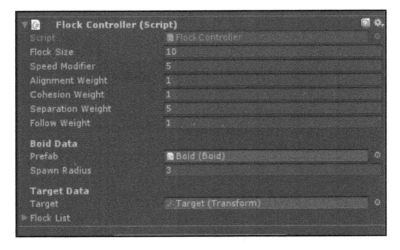

The FlockController component

The preceding screenshot shows the values we have set in the sample scene. As you can see, the separation weight is a bit higher than the rest. Feel free to tweak the weight values in play mode to see how it affects the boids' behavior. Next, let's take a look at the target game object. The following screenshot shows our sample setup:

The test values for our target movement script

The screenshot shows the optimal values for our test scene. Tweaking the bounds might result in some wild camera movement, but play with the move and turn speed to see how it affects the scene in play mode. Lastly, let's take a look at our boid prefab, which has the `Boid` component on it. The provided sample project's boid settings can be seen in the following screenshot:

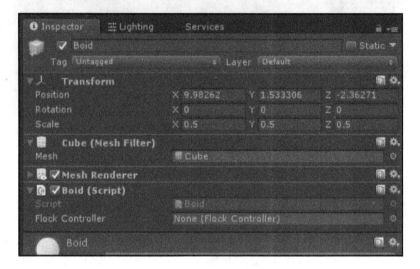

All the components and setup for the Boid game object

There isn't too much excitement in the preceding screenshot. As you can see, the **Flock Controller** is empty (because we assign it via code at runtime), and there are no other values to be tweaked on the boid itself, besides the appearance if you feel so inclined, but our neon green cube is a work of art, if I do say so myself.

When you hit play, you'll see your boids spawn and follow the target as it zooms around the scene. It'll look something like the following screenshot:

Our flock of boids swarming towards the target sphere

And just like that, we've created our very own flocking system. It's highly encouraged that you not only tweak the values in the inspector, but that you take a stab at modifying the code. The easiest way to see how a value affects the entire system is to either remove it, or increase it by a ridiculous amount. Next, we'll take a look at crowds in Unity 2017.

Using crowds

Crowd simulations are far less cut-and-dried. There really isn't any *one* way to implement them in a general sense. While not a strict definition, the term "crowd simulation" generally refers to simulating crowds of humanoid agents navigating an area while avoiding each other and the environment. Like flocks, the use of crowd simulations has been widely used in films. For example, the epic armies of Rohan, Gondor, and Mordor battling one another in *The Lord of the Rings* were completely procedurally generated using the crowd simulation software **Massive**, which was created for use in the film. While the use of crowd algorithms is not as widespread in video games as in films, certain genres rely on the concept more than others. Real-time strategy games often involve armies of characters moving in unison across the screen, and many sandbox games simulate dense cities with many agents on-screen going about their day while avoiding each other, the player, and even traffic.

Implementing a simple crowd simulation

Our implementation will be quick, simple, and effective, and it will focus on using Unity's NavMesh feature. Thankfully, NavMesh will handle much of the heavy lifting for us. Our sample Crowds scene has a simple walking surface with a NavMesh baked onto it, a couple of targets, and two teams of capsules, as shown in the following screenshot:

The classic scenario: red versus blue

In the preceding screenshot, we can see that our red and blue targets are opposite their teams: red and blue, respectively. Your guess is as good as mine as to why the blue and red clans just can't get along, but it'll work for our sample, so I'm just going to let them do their thing. The setup is straightforward. Each capsule has a `CrowdAgent.cs` component attached to it, and when you hit play, each agent will head towards their target while avoiding each other and the oncoming capsules from the opposite team. Once they reach their destination, they will gather around the target.

This setup takes our example from `Chapter 4`, *Finding Your Way* and takes it to the next level. Now we have large groups of agents that are not only navigating to a target location, but doing so while avoiding large groups of agents at the same time. As you can see, Unity's NavMesh handles these interactions beautifully. The system is efficient and very robust.

While the game is running, you can even select a single capsule or a group of them in the editor to see their behavior visualized. As long as you have the navigation window active, you'll be able to see some debugging information about your NavMesh and the agents on it, as you can see in the following screenshot:

The debug view from an agent's perspective

It's worth checking this out in the editor to really get an idea of how this looks in motion, but we've labeled a few key elements in the preceding screenshot:

1. This is the destination arrow that points toward the `NavMeshAgent` destination, which for this little guy is `RedTarget`. All this arrow cares about is where the destination is, regardless of the direction the agent is facing or moving toward.

2. This arrow is the heading arrow. It shows the actual direction the agent is moving in. The direction of the agent takes into account several factors, including the position of its neighbors, space on the NavMesh, and the destination.

3. This debug menu allows you to show a few different things. In our case, we enabled **Show Avoidance** and **Show Neighbours**.

4. Speaking of avoidance, this cluster of squares, ranging from dark to light and floating over the agents, represents the areas to avoid between our agent and the destination. The darker squares indicate areas that are densely populated by other agents or blocked by the environment, while the lighter-white squares indicate areas that are safe to walk through. Of course, this is a dynamic display, so watch it change as you play in the editor.

Using the CrowdAgent component

The CrowdAgent component is incredibly simple, but gets the job done. As mentioned earlier, Unity does most of the heavy lifting for us. The following code gives our CrowdAgent a destination:

```
using UnityEngine;
using System.Collections;

[RequireComponent(typeof(NavMeshAgent))]
public class CrowdAgent : MonoBehaviour
{
    public Transform target;

    private NavMeshAgent agent;

    void Start ()
    {
        agent = GetComponent<NavMeshAgent>();
        agent.speed = Random.Range(4.0f, 5.0f);
        agent.SetDestination(target.position);
    }
}
```

The script requires a component of type `NavMeshAgent`, which it assigns to the `agent` variable on `Start()`. We then set its speed randomly between two values for some added visual variety in our simulation. Lastly, we set its destination to be the position of the target marker. The target marker is assigned via the inspector, as you can see in the following screenshot:

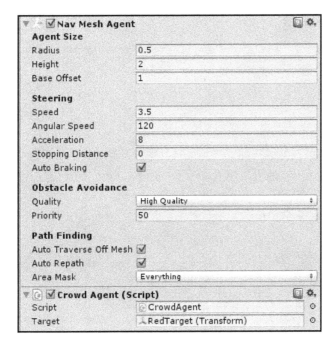

The inspector settings for the NavMeshAgent

The preceding screenshot illustrates a red capsule's `CrowdAgent` component with **RedTarget (Transform)** set as its **Target**. For fun, you can try setting different targets. Since the only requirement is that it be of type `Transform`, you could even set another agent as the target!

Adding some fun obstacles

Without having to do anything else in our code, we can make a few changes to our scene layout and enable a few components provided by Unity to dramatically alter the behavior of our agents. In our `CrowdsObstacles` scene, we've added a few walls to the environment, creating a maze-like layout for our red and blue teams of capsules to traverse, as you can see in the following screenshot:

Let the games begin!

The fun part about this example is that, because of the randomized speed of each agent, the results will be totally different each time you run the game. As the agents move through the environment, they'll be blocked by teammates or opposing agents and will be forced to re-route and find the quickest route to their target. Of course, this concept is not new to us, as we saw NavMeshAgent avoiding obstacles in Chapter 4, *Finding Your Way*, except that we have many, many more agents in this scenario. To add a bit more fun to the example, we've also added a simple up-down animation to one of the walls and a NavMeshObstacle component, which looks something like this:

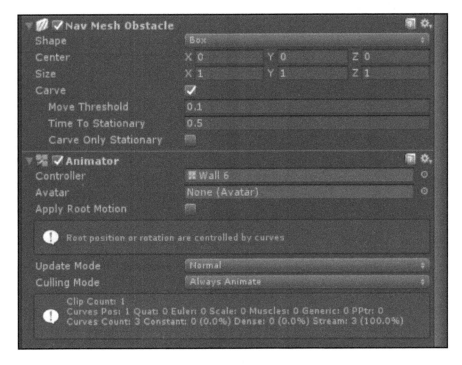

NavMeshObstacle looks a bit different in Unity 2017

Note that our obstacle does not need to be set to **Static** when we are using this component. Our obstacle is mostly box-like, so we leave the default **Shape** setting as **Box** (**Capsule** is another choice). The **Size** and **Center** options let us move the outline of our shape around and resize it, but the default settings fit our shape perfectly, which is what we want, so let's leave that alone. The next option, **Carve**, is important. It essentially does exactly what it says; it carves a space out of the NavMesh, as shown in the following screenshot:

The same obstacle at two different points of its up-down animation

The left screenshot shows the space carved out when the obstacle is on the surface, while the NavMesh is connected in the right screenshot when the obstacle is raised off the surface. We can leave **Time to Stationary** and **Move Threshold** as they are, but we do want to make sure that **Carve Only Stationary** is turned off. This is because our obstacle is moving, and if we didn't tick this box, it would not carve out the space from the NavMesh, and our agents would be trying to move through the obstacle whether it was up or down, which is not the behavior we are after in this case.

As the obstacle moves up and down and the mesh is carved out and reconnected, you'll notice the agents changing their heading. With the navigation debug options enabled, we can also see a very interesting visualization of everything going on with our agents at any given moment. It may seem a bit cruel to mess with our poor agents like this, but we're doing it for science!

The following screenshot gives us a glimpse into the chaos and disorder we're subjecting our poor agents to:

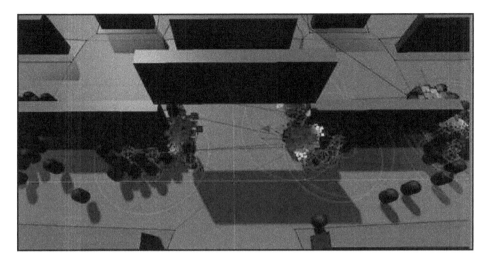

I'm secretly rooting for the blue team

Summary

In this chapter, we learned how to implement a flocking behavior system. We implemented it using custom direction vectors to control the boids' movement that we calculated by applying Craig Reynolds' three main flocking concepts—alignment, coherence, and separation. We then applied our flocking behavior to the flying objects, but you can apply the techniques in these examples to implement other character behaviors, such as fish shoaling, insects swarming, or land animals herding. You'll only have to implement different leader movement behaviors, such as limiting movement along the y axis for characters that can't move up and down. For a 2D game, we would just freeze the y position. For 2D movement along uneven terrain, we would have to modify our script to not put any forces in the y direction.

We also took a look at crowd simulation and even implemented our own version of it using Unity's NavMesh system, which we first learned about in Chapter 4, *Finding Your Way*. We learned how to visualize our agents' behavior and decision-making process.

In the next chapter, we'll look at the behavior tree pattern and learn to implement our own version of it from scratch.

6
Behavior Trees

Behavior trees (**BTs**) have been gaining popularity among game developers very steadily. Over the last decade, BTs have become the pattern of choice for many developers when it comes to implementing behavioral rules for their AI agents. Games such as *Halo* and *Gears of War* are among the more famous franchises to make extensive use of BTs. An abundance of computing power in PCs, gaming consoles, and mobile devices has made them a good option for implementing AI in games of all types and scopes.

In this chapter, we will cover the following topics:

- The basics of a behavior tree
- The benefits of using existing behavior tree solutions
- How to implement our own behavior tree framework
- How to implement a basic tree using our framework

Technical Requirements

You will be required to have Unity 2017 installed on a system that has either Windows 7 SP1+, 8, 10, 64-bit versions or Mac OS X 10.9+. The code in this book will not run on Windows XP and Vista, and server versions of Windows and OS X are not tested.

The code files of this chapter can be found on GitHub:
`https://github.com/PacktPublishing/Unity-2017-Game-AI-Programming-Third-Edition/tree/master/Chapter06`

Check out the following video to see the code in action:
`https://goo.gl/FrcGNT`

Learning the basics of behavior trees

Behavior trees got their name from their hierarchical, branching system of nodes with a common parent, known as the root. As you've surely learned by now from reading this book, behavior trees too mimic the real thing they are named after—in this case, trees and their branching structure. If we were to visualize a behavior tree, it would look something like the following figure:

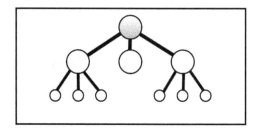

A basic tree structure

Of course, behavior trees can be made up of any number of nodes and child nodes. The nodes at the very end of the hierarchy are referred to as leaf nodes, just like a tree. Nodes can represent behaviors or tests. Unlike state machines, which rely on transition rules to traverse through them, a BT's flow is defined strictly by each node's order within the larger hierarchy. A BT begins evaluating from the top of the tree (based on the preceding visualization), then continues through each child, which, in turn, runs through each of its children until a condition is met or the leaf node is reached. BTs always begin evaluating from the root node.

Understanding different node types

The names of the different types of node may vary depending on who you ask, and even nodes themselves are sometimes referred to as tasks. While the complexity of a tree is dependent entirely upon the needs of the AI, the high-level concepts about how BTs work are fairly easy to understand if we look at each component individually. The following is true for each node regardless of what type of node we're referring to. A node will always return one of the following states:

- **Success**: The condition the node was checking for has been met.
- **Failure**: The condition the node was checking for was not, and will not, be met.
- **Running**: The validity of the condition the node is checking for has not been determined. Think of this as our "please wait" state.

Due to the potential complexity of a BT, most implementations are asynchronous, which, at least for Unity, means that evaluating a tree will not block the game from continuing other operations. The evaluation process of the various nodes in a BT can take several frames, if necessary. If you had to evaluate several trees on any number of agents at a time, you can imagine how it would negatively affect the performance of the program to have to wait for each of them to return a true or false to the root node. This is why the "running" state is important.

Defining composite nodes

Composite nodes are called so as they have one or more children. Their state is based entirely upon the result of evaluating their children, and while their children are being evaluated, they will be in a "running" state. There are a couple of composite node types, which are mostly defined by how their children are evaluated:

- **Sequences**: The defining characteristic of a sequence is that the entire sequence of children needs to complete successfully in order for it to evaluate as a success itself. If any of the children at any step of the sequence return false, the sequence itself will report a failure. It is important to note that, in general, sequences are executed from left to right.

The following figures show a successful sequence and a failed sequence, respectively:

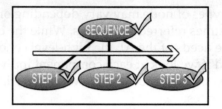

A successful sequence node

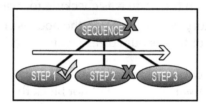

An unsuccessful sequence node

- **Selectors**: By comparison, selectors are much more forgiving parents to their children nodes. If any one of the children nodes in a selector sequence returns true, the selector says, "eh, good enough!" and returns true immediately, without evaluating any more of its children. The only way a selector node will return false is if all of its children are evaluated and none of them return a success.

Of course, each composite node type has its use depending on the situation. You can think of the different types of sequence nodes as "and" and "or" conditionals.

Understanding decorator nodes

The biggest difference between a composite node and a decorator node is that a decorator can have exactly one child, and one child only. At first, this may seem unnecessary as you would, in theory, be able to get the same functionality by containing the condition in the node itself rather than relying on its child, but the decorator node is special in that it essentially takes the state returned by the child and evaluates the response based on its own parameters. A decorator can even specify how its children are evaluated and how often they are evaluated. These are some common decorator types:

- **Inverter**: Think of the inverter as a NOT modifier. It takes the opposite of the state returned by its child. For example, if the child returns TRUE, the decorator evaluates as FALSE, and vice versa. This is the equivalent of having the ! operator in front of a Boolean in C#.
- **Repeater**: This repeats the evaluation of the child a specified (or infinite) number of times until it evaluates as either TRUE or FALSE as determined by the decorator. For example, you may want to wait indefinitely until a certain condition is met, such as "having enough energy" before a character uses an attack.
- **Limiter**: This simply limits the number of times a node will be evaluated to avoid getting an agent stuck in an awkward infinite behavior loop. This decorator, in contrast to the repeater, can be used to make sure a character only tries to, for example, kick the door open so many times before giving up and trying something else.

Some decorator nodes can be used for debugging and testing your trees, for example:

- **Fake state**: This always evaluates true or false as specified by the decorator. This is very helpful for asserting certain behavior in your agent. For example, you can also have the decorator maintain a fake "running" state indefinitely to see how other agents around it will behave.
- **Breakpoint**: Just like a breakpoint in code, you can have this node fire off logic to notify you via debug logs or other methods that the node has been reached.

These types are not monolithic archetypes that are mutually exclusive. You can combine these types of nodes to suit your needs. Just be careful not to combine too much functionality into one decorator to the point where it may be more efficient or convenient to use a sequence node instead.

Describing the leaf node

We briefly covered leaf nodes earlier in the chapter to make a point about the structure of a BT, but leaf nodes, in reality, can be just about any sort of behavior. They are magical in the sense that they can be used to describe any sort of logic your agent can have. A leaf node can specify a walk function, shoot command, or kick action. It doesn't matter what it does or how you decide to have it evaluate its states, it just has to be the last node in its own hierarchy and return any of the three states a node can return.

Evaluating the existing solutions

The Unity asset store is an excellent resource for developers. Not only are you able to purchase art, audio, and other kinds of assets, but it is also populated with a large number of plugins and frameworks. Most relevant to our purposes, there are a number of behavior tree plugins available on the asset store, ranging from free to a few hundred dollars. Most, if not all, provide some sort of GUI to make visualizing and arranging a fairly painless experience.

There are many advantages of going with an off-the-shelf solution from the asset store. Many of the frameworks include advanced functionality such as runtime (and often visual) debugging, robust APIs, serialization, and data-oriented tree support. Many even include sample leaf logic nodes to use in your game, minimizing the amount of coding you have to do to get up and running.

The previous edition of this book, *Unity 4.x Game AI Programming*, focused on developer AngryAnt's Behave plugin, which is currently available as Behave 2 for Unity on the asset store as a paid plugin, which continues to be an excellent choice for your behavior tree needs (and so much more). It is a very robust, performant, and excellently designed framework.

Some other alternatives are **Behavior Machine** and **Behavior Designer**, which offer different pricing tiers (Behavior Machine even offers a free edition) and a wide array of useful features. Many other options can be found for free around the web as both generic C# and Unity-specific implementations. Ultimately, as with any other system, the choice of rolling your own or using an existing solution will depend on your time, budget, and project.

Implementing a basic behavior tree framework

While a fully-fledged implementation of a behavior tree with a GUI and its many node types and variations is outside the scope of this book, we can certainly focus on the core principles to get a solid grasp of what the concepts we've covered in this chapter look like in action. Provided with this chapter is the basic framework for a behavior tree. Our example will focus on simple logic to highlight the functionality of the tree, rather than muddy up the example with complex game logic. The goal of our example is to make you feel comfortable with what can seem like an intimidating concept in game AI, and give you the necessary tools to build your own tree and expand upon the provided code if you do so.

Implementing a base Node class

There is a base functionality that needs to go into every node. Our simple framework will have all the nodes derived from a base abstract `Node.cs` class. This class will provide said base functionality or at least the signature to expand upon that functionality:

```
using UnityEngine;
using System.Collections;

[System.Serializable]
public abstract class Node {

    /* Delegate that returns the state of the node.*/
    public delegate NodeStates NodeReturn();

    /* The current state of the node */
    protected NodeStates m_nodeState;

    public NodeStates nodeState {
        get { return m_nodeState; }
    }

    /* The constructor for the node */
    public Node() {}

    /* Implementing classes use this method to evaluate the desired set of
conditions */
    public abstract NodeStates Evaluate();

}
```

The class is fairly simple. Think of `Node.cs` as a blueprint for all the other node types to be built upon. We begin with the `NodeReturn` delegate, which is not implemented in our example, but the next two fields are. However, `m_nodeState` is the state of a node at any given point. As we learned earlier, it will be either FAILURE, SUCCESS, or RUNNING. The `nodeState` value is simply a getter for `m_nodeState` since it is protected and we don't want any other area of the code directly setting `m_nodeState` inadvertently.

Next, we have an empty constructor, for the sake of being explicit, even though it is not being used. Lastly, we have the meat and potatoes of our `Node.cs` class—the `Evaluate()` method. As we'll see in the classes that implement `Node.cs`, `Evaluate()` is where the magic happens. It runs the code that determines the state of the node.

Extending nodes to selectors

To create a selector, we simply expand upon the functionality that we described in the
Node.cs class:

```
using UnityEngine;
using System.Collections;
using System.Collections.Generic;

public class Selector : Node {
    /** The child nodes for this selector */
    protected List<Node> m_nodes = new List<Node>();


    /** The constructor requires a lsit of child nodes to be
     * passed in*/
    public Selector(List<Node> nodes) {
        m_nodes = nodes;
    }

    /* If any of the children reports a success, the selector will
     * immediately report a success upwards. If all children fail,
     * it will report a failure instead.*/
    public override NodeStates Evaluate() {
        foreach (Node node in m_nodes) {
            switch (node.Evaluate()) {
                case NodeStates.FAILURE:
                    continue;
                case NodeStates.SUCCESS:
                    m_nodeState = NodeStates.SUCCESS;
                    return m_nodeState;
                case NodeStates.RUNNING:
                    m_nodeState = NodeStates.RUNNING;
                    return m_nodeState;
                default:
                    continue;
            }
        }
        m_nodeState = NodeStates.FAILURE;
        return m_nodeState;
    }
}
```

As we learned earlier in the chapter, selectors are composite nodes: this means that they have one or more child nodes. These child nodes are stored in the `m_nodes List<Node>` variable. Although it's conceivable that one could extend the functionality of this class to allow adding more child nodes after the class has been instantiated, we initially provide this list via the constructor.

The next portion of the code is a bit more interesting as it shows us a real implementation of the concepts we learned earlier. The `Evaluate()` method runs through all of its child nodes and evaluates each one individually. As a failure doesn't necessarily mean a failure for the entire selector, if one of the children returns `FAILURE`, we simply continue on to the next one. Inversely, if any child returns `SUCCESS`, then we're all set; we can set this node's state accordingly and return that value. If we make it through the entire list of child nodes and none of them have returned `SUCCESS`, then we can essentially determine that the entire selector has failed and we assign and return a `FAILURE` state.

Moving on to sequences

Sequences are very similar in their implementation, but as you might have guessed by now, the `Evaluate()` method behaves differently:

```
using UnityEngine;
using System.Collections;
using System.Collections.Generic;

public class Sequence : Node {
    /** Children nodes that belong to this sequence */
    private List<Node> m_nodes = new List<Node>();

    /** Must provide an initial set of children nodes to work */
    public Sequence(List<Node> nodes) {
        m_nodes = nodes;
    }

    /* If any child node returns a failure, the entire node fails. Whence
all
     * nodes return a success, the node reports a success. */
    public override NodeStates Evaluate() {
        bool anyChildRunning = false;
        foreach(Node node in m_nodes) {
            switch (node.Evaluate()) {
                case NodeStates.FAILURE:
                    m_nodeState = NodeStates.FAILURE;
                    return m_nodeState;
```

```
                    case NodeStates.SUCCESS:
                        continue;
                    case NodeStates.RUNNING:
                        anyChildRunning = true;
                        continue;
                    default:
                        m_nodeState = NodeStates.SUCCESS;
                        return m_nodeState;
                }
            }
            m_nodeState = anyChildRunning ? NodeStates.RUNNING :
        NodeStates.SUCCESS;
            return m_nodeState;
        }
    }
```

The `Evaluate()` method in a sequence will need to return true for all the child nodes, and if any one of them fails during the process, the entire sequence fails, which is why we check for `FAILURE` first and set and report it accordingly. A `SUCCESS` state simply means we get to live to fight another day, and we continue on to the next child node. If any of the child nodes are determined to be in the `RUNNING` state, we report that as the state for the node, and then the parent node or the logic driving the entire tree can evaluate it again.

Implementing a decorator as an inverter

The structure of `Inverter.cs` is a bit different, but it derives from `Node`, just like the rest of the nodes. Let's take a look at the code and spot the differences:

```
using UnityEngine;
using System.Collections;

public class Inverter : Node {
    /* Child node to evaluate */
    private Node m_node;

    public Node node {
        get { return m_node; }
    }

    /* The constructor requires the child node that this inverter decorator
     * wraps*/
    public Inverter(Node node) {
        m_node = node;
    }
```

```
    /* Reports a success if the child fails and
     * a failure if the child succeeds. Running will report
     * as running */
    public override NodeStates Evaluate() {
        switch (m_node.Evaluate()) {
            case NodeStates.FAILURE:
                m_nodeState = NodeStates.SUCCESS;
                return m_nodeState;
            case NodeStates.SUCCESS:
                m_nodeState = NodeStates.FAILURE;
                return m_nodeState;
            case NodeStates.RUNNING:
                m_nodeState = NodeStates.RUNNING;
                return m_nodeState;
        }
        m_nodeState = NodeStates.SUCCESS;
        return m_nodeState;
    }
}
```

As you can see, since a decorator only has one child, we don't have List<Node>, but rather a single node variable, m_node. We pass this node in via the constructor (essentially requiring it), but there is no reason you couldn't modify this code to provide an empty constructor and a method to assign the child node after instantiation.

The Evalute() implementation implements the behavior of an inverter that we described earlier in the chapter: when the child evaluates as SUCCESS, the inverter reports a FAILURE, and when the child evaluates as FAILURE, the inverter reports a SUCCESS. The RUNNING state is reported normally.

Creating a generic action node

Now we arrive at ActionNode.cs, which is a generic leaf node to pass in some logic via a delegate. You are free to implement leaf nodes in any way that fits your logic, as long as it derives from Node. This particular example is equal parts flexible and restrictive. It's flexible in the sense that it allows you to pass in any method matching the delegate signature, but is restrictive for this very reason—it only provides one delegate signature that doesn't take in any arguments:

```
using System;
using UnityEngine;
using System.Collections;

public class ActionNode : Node {
```

```
/* Method signature for the action. */
public delegate NodeStates ActionNodeDelegate();

/* The delegate that is called to evaluate this node */
private ActionNodeDelegate m_action;

/* Because this node contains no logic itself,
 * the logic must be passed in in the form of
 * a delegate. As the signature states, the action
 * needs to return a NodeStates enum */
public ActionNode(ActionNodeDelegate action) {
    m_action = action;
}

/* Evaluates the node using the passed in delegate and
 * reports the resulting state as appropriate */
public override NodeStates Evaluate() {
    switch (m_action()) {
        case NodeStates.SUCCESS:
            m_nodeState = NodeStates.SUCCESS;
            return m_nodeState;
        case NodeStates.FAILURE:
            m_nodeState = NodeStates.FAILURE;
            return m_nodeState;
        case NodeStates.RUNNING:
            m_nodeState = NodeStates.RUNNING;
            return m_nodeState;
        default:
            m_nodeState = NodeStates.FAILURE;
            return m_nodeState;
    }
}
}
```

The key for making this node work is the `m_action` delegate. For those familiar with C++, a delegate in C# can be thought of as a function pointer of sorts. You can also think of a delegate as a variable containing (or more accurately, pointing to) a function. This allows you to set the function to be called at runtime. The constructor requires you to pass in a method matching its signature, and is expecting that method to return a `NodeStates` enum. That method can implement any logic you want, as long as these conditions are met. Unlike other nodes we've implemented, this one doesn't fall through to any state outside of the switch itself, so it defaults to a `FAILURE` state. You may choose to default to a `SUCCESS` or `RUNNING` state, if you so wish, by modifying the default return.

You can easily expand on this class by deriving from it or simply making the changes to it that you need. You can also skip this generic action node altogether and implement one-off versions of specific leaf nodes, but it's good practice to reuse as much code as possible. Just remember to derive from `Node` and implement the required code!

Testing our framework

The framework that we just reviewed is nothing more than this. It provides us with all the functionality we need to make a tree, but we have to make the actual tree ourselves. For the purposes of this book, a somewhat manually constructed tree is provided.

Planning ahead

Before we set up our tree, let's look at what we're trying to accomplish. It is often helpful to visualize a tree before implementing it. Our tree will count up from zero to a specified value. Along the way, it will check whether certain conditions are met for that value and report its state accordingly. The following diagram illustrates the basic hierarchy for our tree:

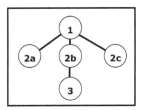

For our tests, we will use a three-tier tree, including the root node:

- **Node 1**: This is our root node. It has children, and we want to be able to return a success if any of the children are a success, so we'll implement it as a selector.
- **Node 2a**: We'll implement this node using an `ActionNode`.
- **Node 2b**: We'll use this node to demonstrate how our inverter works.
- **Node 2c**: We'll run the same `ActionNode` from node **2a** again, and see how that affects our tree's evaluation.
- **Node 3**: Node **3** happens to be the lone node in the third tier of the tree. It is the child of the **2b** decorator node. This means that if it reports SUCCESS, **2b** will report a FAILURE, and vice versa.

At this point, we're still a bit vague on the implementation details, but the preceding diagram will help us to visualize our tree as we implement it in code. Keep it handy for reference as we go through the code.

Examining our scene setup

We've now looked at the basic structure of our tree, and before we jump in and dig into the actual code implementation, let's look at our scene setup. The following screenshot shows our hierarchy; the nodes are highlighted for emphasis:

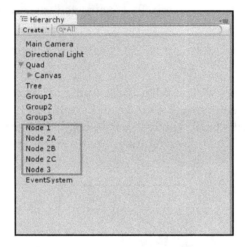

The setup is quite simple. There is a quad with a world-space canvas, which is simply to display some information during the test. The nodes highlighted in the preceding screenshot will be referenced in the code later, and we'll be using them to visualize the status of each individual node. The actual scene looks something like the following screenshot:

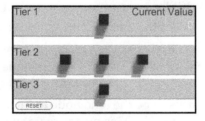

Our actual layout mimics the diagram we created earlier

As you can see, we have one node or box representing each of the nodes that we laid out in our planning phase. These are referenced in the actual test code and will be changing colors according to the state that is returned.

Exploring the MathTree code

Without further ado, let's have a look at the code driving our test. This is `MathTree.cs`:

```
using UnityEngine;
using UnityEngine.UI;
using System.Collections;
using System.Collections.Generic;

public class MathTree : MonoBehaviour {
    public Color m_evaluating;
    public Color m_succeeded;
    public Color m_failed;

    public Selector m_rootNode;

    public ActionNode m_node2A;
    public Inverter m_node2B;
    public ActionNode m_node2C;
    public ActionNode m_node3;

    public GameObject m_rootNodeBox;
    public GameObject m_node2aBox;
    public GameObject m_node2bBox;
    public GameObject m_node2cBox;
    public GameObject m_node3Box;

    public  int m_targetValue = 20;
    private int m_currentValue = 0;

    [SerializeField]
    private Text m_valueLabel;
```

The first few variables are simply used for debugging. The three color variables are the colors we'll be assigning to our node boxes to visualize their state. By default, RUNNING is yellow, SUCCESS is green, and FAILED is red. This is pretty standard stuff; let's move along.

We then declare our actual nodes. As you can see, `m_rootNode` is a selector, as we mentioned earlier. Notice that we do not assign any of the node variables yet, since we have to pass in some data to their constructors.

We then have the references to the boxes we saw in our scene. These are just game objects that we drag and drop into the inspector (we'll have a look at that after we inspect the code).

We then have a couple of `int` values, which will make more sense as we look at the logic, so we'll skip over these. Lastly, we have a unity UI Text variable that will display some values for us during the test.

Let's get into the initialization of our actual nodes:

```
    /* We instantiate our nodes from the bottom up, and assign the children
     * in that order */
  void Start () {
        /** The deepest-level node is Node 3, which has no children. */
        m_node3 = new ActionNode(NotEqualToTarget);

        /** Next up, we create the level 2 nodes. */
        m_node2A = new ActionNode(AddTen);

        /** Node 2B is a selector which has node 3 as a child, so we'll
pass
         * node 3 to the constructor */
        m_node2B = new Inverter(m_node3);

        m_node2C = new ActionNode(AddTen);

        /** Lastly, we have our root node. First, we prepare our list of
children
         * nodes to pass in */
        List<Node> rootChildren = new List<Node>();
        rootChildren.Add(m_node2A);
        rootChildren.Add(m_node2B);
        rootChildren.Add(m_node2C);

        /** Then we create our root node object and pass in the list */
        m_rootNode = new Selector(rootChildren);

        m_valueLabel.text = m_currentValue.ToString();

        m_rootNode.Evaluate();

        UpdateBoxes();
    }
```

For the sake of organization, we declare our nodes from the bottom of the tree to the top of the tree, or the root node. We do this because we cannot instantiate a parent without passing in its child nodes, so we have to instantiate the child nodes first. Notice that m_node2A, m_node2C, and m_node3 are action nodes, so we pass in delegates (we'll look at these methods next). Then, m_node2B, being a selector, takes in a node as a child, in this case m_node3. After we've declared these tiers, we throw all the tier 2 nodes into a list because our tier 1 node, the root node, is a selector that requires a list of children to be instantiated.

After we've instantiated all of our nodes, we kick off the process and begin evaluating our root node using its Evaluate() method. The UpdateBoxes() method simply updates the box game objects that we declared earlier with the appropriate colors; we'll look at that later on in this section:

```
private void UpdateBoxes() {
        /** Update root node box */
        if (m_rootNode.nodeState == NodeStates.SUCCESS) {
            SetSucceeded(m_rootNodeBox);
        } else if (m_rootNode.nodeState == NodeStates.FAILURE) {
            SetFailed(m_rootNodeBox);
        }

        /** Update 2A node box */
        if (m_node2A.nodeState == NodeStates.SUCCESS) {
            SetSucceeded(m_node2aBox);
        } else if (m_node2A.nodeState == NodeStates.FAILURE) {
            SetFailed(m_node2aBox);
        }

        /** Update 2B node box */
        if (m_node2B.nodeState == NodeStates.SUCCESS) {
            SetSucceeded(m_node2bBox);
        } else if (m_node2B.nodeState == NodeStates.FAILURE) {
            SetFailed(m_node2bBox);
        }

        /** Update 2C node box */
        if (m_node2C.nodeState == NodeStates.SUCCESS) {
            SetSucceeded(m_node2cBox);
        } else if (m_node2C.nodeState == NodeStates.FAILURE) {
            SetFailed(m_node2cBox);
        }

        /** Update 3 node box */
        if (m_node3.nodeState == NodeStates.SUCCESS) {
            SetSucceeded(m_node3Box);
```

```
        } else if (m_node3.nodeState == NodeStates.FAILURE) {
            SetFailed(m_node3Box);
        }
    }
```

There is not a whole lot to discuss here. Do notice that, because we set this tree up manually, we check each node individually and get its `nodeState` and set the colors using the `SetSucceeded` and `SetFailed` methods. Let's move on to the meaty part of the class:

```
    private NodeStates NotEqualToTarget() {
        if (m_currentValue != m_targetValue) {
            return NodeStates.SUCCESS;
        } else {
            return NodeStates.FAILURE;
        }
    }

    private NodeStates AddTen() {
        m_currentValue += 10;
        m_valueLabel.text = m_currentValue.ToString();
        if (m_currentValue == m_targetValue) {
            return NodeStates.SUCCESS;
        } else {
            return NodeStates.FAILURE;
        }
    }
```

First, we have `NotEqualToTarget()`, which is the method we passed into our decorator's child action node. We're essentially setting ourselves up for a double negative here, so try to follow along. This method returns a success if the current value is *not* equal to the target value, and returns false otherwise. The parent inverter decorator will then evaluate to the opposite of what this node returns. So, if the value is not equal, the inverter node will fail; otherwise, it will succeed. If you're feeling a bit lost at this point, don't worry. It will all make sense when we see this in action.

The next method is the `AddTen()` method, which is the method passed into our other two action nodes. It does exactly what the name implies—it adds 10 to our `m_currentValue` variable, then checks whether it's equal to our `m_targetValue`, and evaluates as `SUCCESS` if so, and `FAILURE` if not.

The last few methods are self-explanatory so we will not go over them.

Executing the test

Now that we have a pretty good idea of how the code works, let's see it in action. First things first, however. Let's make sure our component is properly set up. Select the **Tree** game object from the hierarchy, and its inspector should look similar to this:

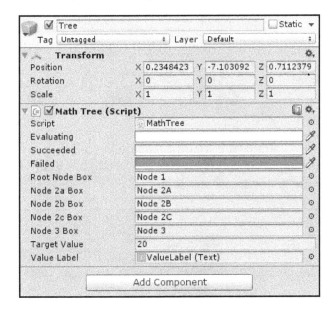

The default settings for the component

As you can see, the state colors and box references have already been assigned for you, as well as the `m_valueLabel` variable. The `m_targetValue` variable has also been assigned for you via code. Make sure to leave it at (or set it to) 20 before you hit play. Play the scene, and you'll see your boxes lit up, as shown in the following screenshot:

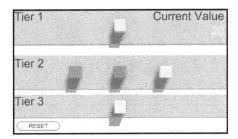

The boxes lit up, indicating the result of each node's evaluation

As we can see, our root node evaluated to SUCCESS, which is what we intended, but let's examine why, one step at a time, starting at tier 2:

- **Node 2A**: We started with m_currentValue at 0, so upon adding 10 to it, it's still not equal to our m_targetValue (20) and it fails. Thus, it is red.
- **Node 2B**: As it evaluates its child, once again, m_currentValue and m_targetValue are not equal. This returns SUCCESS. Then, the inverter logic kicks in and reverses this response so that it reports FAILURE for itself. So, we move on to the last node.
- **Node 2C**: Once again, we add 10 to m_currentValue. It then becomes 20, which is equal to m_targetValue, and evaluates as SUCCESS, so our root node is successful as a result.

The test is simple, but it illustrates the concepts clearly. Before we consider the test a success, let's run it one more time, but change m_targetValue first. Set it to 30 in the inspector, as shown in the following screenshot:

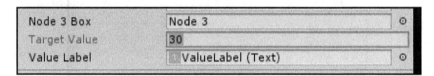

The updated value is highlighted

A small change, to be sure, but it will change how the entire tree evaluates. Play the scene again, and we will end up with the set of nodes lit up, as shown in the following screenshot:

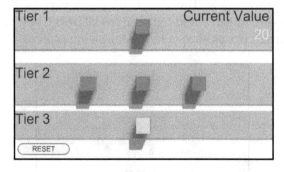

A clearly different result from our first test

As you can see, all but one of the child nodes of our root failed, so it reports FAILURE for itself. Let's look at why:

- **Node 2A**: Nothing really changes here from our original example. Our m_currentValue variable starts at 0 and ends up at 10, which is not equal to our m_targetValue of 30, so it fails.
- **Node 2B**: This evaluates its child once more, and because the child node reports SUCCESS, it reports FAILURE for itself, and we move on to the next node.
- **Node 2C**: Once again, we add 10 to our m_currentValue variable, adding up to 20, which, after having changed the m_targetValue variable, no longer evaluates to SUCCESS.

The current implementation of the nodes will have unevaluated nodes default to SUCCESS. This is because of our enum order, as you can see in NodeState.cs:

```
public enum NodeStates {
    SUCCESS,
    FAILURE,
    RUNNING,
}
```

In our enum, SUCCESS is the first enumeration, so if a node never gets evaluated, the default value is never changed. If you were to change the m_targetValue variable to 10, for example, all the nodes would light up to green. This is simply a by-product of our test implementation and doesn't actually reflect any design issues with our nodes. Our UpdateBoxes() method updates all the boxes whether they were evaluated or not. In this example, node **2A** would immediately evaluate as SUCCESS, which, in turn, would cause the root node to report SUCCESS, and neither node **2B**, **2C**, nor **3** would be evaluated at all, having no effect on the evaluation of the tree as a whole.

You are highly encouraged to play with this test. Change the root node implementation from a selector to a sequence, for example. By simply changing public Selector m_rootNode; to public Sequence m_rootNode; and m_rootNode = new Selector(rootChildren); to m_rootNode = new Sequence(rootChildren);, you can test a completely different set of functionality.

HomeRock card game example

To further illustrate potential uses for BTs, let's take a look at the second example for this chapter included in the sample code. In the `CardGame` Unity scene, you'll find an implementation of a turn-based card game, where the player and the AI opponent have three different abilities: attack, heal, and defend. The user gets to pick which ability to use on their turn, and the AI will use a BT to decide which course of action to take. The game ends when a player reaches 0 hit points. The following image illustrates our game view:

Game screen for HomeRock—Heroes of Unity

As you can see here, the player can select their attack by clicking on one of the cards, which have been spruced up with some flavor text. The player's hit points are displayed in the lower-left corner, and the AI enemy's hit points are displayed in the top-right corner of the screen. The premise is simple, even if the example is a bit silly. Let's take a look at the scene setup before we dive into the code.

The scene setup

There are quite a few things going on in this scene, as this example is a bit more complex than previous ones in this book. We'll touch on each element, but will keep our focus on the topic at hand: behavior trees. Let's take a look at the scene hierarchy, which looks like the following screenshot:

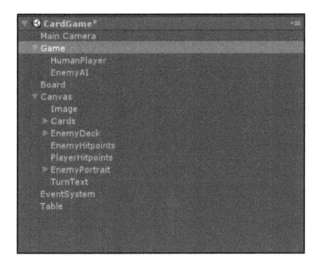

The scene hierarchy

In the hierarchy depicted in this screenshot, we'll find a few game-related elements, and you may also notice that the canvas has quite a few elements nested under it.

The **Game** game object has two components on it—the Animator, which controls the game states, and the `Game.cs` component, which controls the game flow and rules. First, let's take a look at the game states. The Animator has a reference to the `GameFlowStateMachine`, which looks like this screenshot:

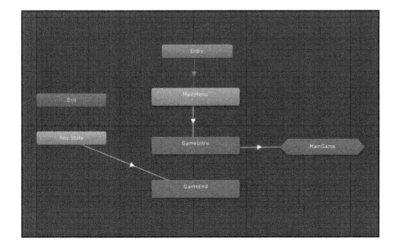

The state machine depicted has a few boilerplate states, such as **MainMenu** and **GameEnd**. You'll notice that **MainMenu** is our entry point. While our sample doesn't have a main menu, you could use this state to implement your own. In the sample, the state just automatically transitions to the **GameIntro** state. Again, **GameIntro** is provided as a staging area for you to implement any intro sequences or animations, but defaults to transitioning to the next stage, **MainGame**. Finally, we have **GameEnd**, which you can transition to from any state, so long as you hit the `EndGame` trigger. You may have noticed that **MainGame** is a nested tree, and if we double-click on it to dive into its contents, we'll find a tree that looks like this screenshot:

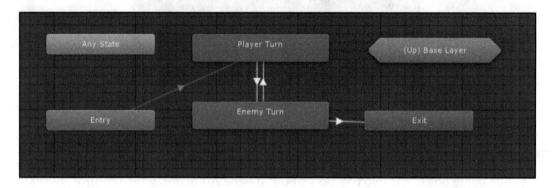

The setup shown in the previous screenshot is simple enough—there is a player turn and an enemy turn. These simply bounce back and forth whenever we set the `EndTurn` trigger. Next, we have our `Game.cs` component, which looks like this in the inspector:

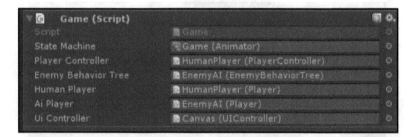

In the previous screenshot, we can see that the **Game** component has some references to other scripts in our scene. We'll get to those in a minute, but do notice that there is a reference to our state machine. Let's dive into the `Game.cs` code to see what's going on under the hood:

```
using UnityEngine;

public class Game : MonoBehaviour {
```

```
[SerializeField]
private Animator stateMachine;
[SerializeField]
private PlayerController playerController;
[SerializeField]
private EnemyBehaviorTree enemyBehaviorTree;
[SerializeField]
private Player humanPlayer;
[SerializeField]
private Player aiPlayer;
[SerializeField]
private UIController uiController;
private int turn = 0;

private void Awake() {
    enemyBehaviorTree.SetPlayerData(humanPlayer, aiPlayer);
    enemyBehaviorTree.onTreeExecuted += EndTurn;
    playerController.onActionExecuted += EndTurn;
}

public void EvaluateAITree() {
    enemyBehaviorTree.Evaluate();
}

private void EndTurn() {
    if(humanPlayer.CurrentHealth <= 0 || aiPlayer.CurrentHealth <= 0) {
        stateMachine.SetTrigger("EndGame");
        uiController.EndGame();
        return;
    }
    stateMachine.SetTrigger("EndTurn");
    turn ^= 1;
    uiController.SetTurn(turn);
}
}
```

First, we have all the serialized values we saw in the inspector just a moment ago, along with a private, non-serialized value, the turn value. This value flips between 0 and 1 for the player's turn and the AI's turn, respectively. Our Awake method does some setup, it initializes values in the EnemyBehaviorTree.cs script, and it adds some callbacks to the enemy AI controller and our player controller.

The `EvaluateAITree()` method simply wraps the enemy's BT's `Evaluate()` method. We do this for some pseudo-decoupling. Lastly, the `EndTurn()` method does a few things: it checks whether either of the players' health is below 0, and ends the game if so; it also toggles the turn value, sets the appropriate trigger on the state machine, and updates the turn message on the `UIController`.

Next in our scene's hierarchy, nested under the **Game** game object, we have a **HumanPlayer** game object, and an **EnemyAI** game object. Both have a `Player.cs` script, which simply contains data and methods that control that player's values. The screenshot here shows the values for the **HumanPlayer** game object's **Player** component:

In order to get a better idea of what the values shown in the preceding screenshot do, let's take a look at the `Player.cs` script and break it down:

```
using UnityEngine;

public class Player : MonoBehaviour {
    [SerializeField]
    private int maxHealth = 20;

    [SerializeField]
    private int currentHealth;

    [SerializeField]
    private int lowHealthThreshold = 7;

    [Header("Ability Parameters")]
    private int minHealAmount = 2;
    private int maxHealAmount = 5;

    private int minDamage = 2;
    private int maxDamage = 5;

    private bool isBuffed = false;

    public int CurrentHealth {
        get { return currentHealth; }
    }
```

```
    public bool IsBuffed {
        get { return isBuffed; }
    }

    public bool HasLowHealth {
        get { return currentHealth < lowHealthThreshold; }
    }

    private void Awake() {
        currentHealth = maxHealth;
    }

    public bool Buff() {
        isBuffed = true;
        return isBuffed;
    }

    public int Heal() {
        int healAmount = Random.Range(minHealAmount, maxHealAmount);
        currentHealth += healAmount;
        return currentHealth;
    }

    public int Damage() {
        int damageAmount = Random.Range(minDamage, maxDamage);
        if(isBuffed) {
            damageAmount /= 2;
            isBuffed = false;
        }
        currentHealth -= damageAmount;
        return currentHealth;
    }
}
```

The first few values are fairly simple. We have the player's max health represented by maxHealth and their current health represented by currentHealth. We use a value called lowHealthThreshold for the AI to make some decisions. It gives us the ability to modify the AI's behavior based on its or its opponent's health.

We then list out some ability parameters. The minHealAmount and maxHealAmount represent the healing ability's lower and upper limits, respectively. The same goes for the minDamage and maxDamage fields for the attack ability. In the case of isBuffed, we use a bool to represent whether or not the player is "buffed," which is a generic term in some game genres to denote that a character or player has a beneficial gameplay status. There are some properties and initialization in our Awake method, and then a series of ability methods.

The Buff() method simply sets the isBuffed value to true. We use this in our damage calculation later on. The Heal() method picks a random number between the range specified by minHealAmount and maxHealAmount, and restores that much health to the player's currentHealth value. Lastly, the Damage() method applies a random amount of damage to the player (by subtracting from its current health), which is halved when the player's isBuffed flag is set to true.

We can now take a look at the next component of the **HumanPlayer** game object, the PlayerController.cs script. The component's inspector values can be seen in the following screenshot:

The inspector showing all the assigned values for the player controller

You'll notice some references to its own Player.cs component as well as the enemy AI's component. The **Buttons** section contains references to the ability card's UI buttons. The code for the class looks like this:

```
using UnityEngine;
using UnityEngine.UI;

public class PlayerController : MonoBehaviour {
    [SerializeField]
    private Player ownData;
    [SerializeField]
    private Player enemyData;

    [Header("Buttons")]
    [SerializeField]
    private Button defendButton;
    [SerializeField]
    private Button healButton;
    [SerializeField]
    private Button attackButton;

    public delegate void ActionExecuted();
```

```
        public event ActionExecuted onActionExecuted;

    void Awake () {
            defendButton.onClick.AddListener(Defend);
            healButton.onClick.AddListener(Heal);
            attackButton.onClick.AddListener(Attack);
    }

    private void Attack() {
        enemyData.Damage();
        EndTurn();
    }

    private void Heal() {
        ownData.Heal();
        EndTurn();
    }
    private void Defend() {
        ownData.Buff();
        EndTurn();
    }

    private void EndTurn() {
        if(onActionExecuted != null) {
            onActionExecuted();
        }
    }
}
```

The variables up top are fairly straightforward, and they are the very values we just saw in the inspector. You'll also find an onActionExecuted event here, which, if you remember, gets assigned from the Game.cs script's Awake() function. In this class's Awake(), we assign an onClick handler for each of the buttons: **Defend**, **Heal**, and **Attack**. Each of the methods calls the appropriate ability method on the Player.cs script, and then calls EndTurn(), which, in turn, calls the onActionExecuted callback. Refer back to the Game.cs script for what that does.

The enemy state machine

The EnemyAI game object has its own Player.cs script, as we saw earlier, but it also has the script we're most interested in: the EnemyBehaviorTree.cs component. This component contains the BT for our enemy agent, along with some helper functionality. Let's take a look at that code now:

```
using UnityEngine;
using System.Collections;
using System.Collections.Generic;

public class EnemyBehaviorTree : MonoBehaviour {
    private Player playerData;
    private Player ownData;

    public RandomBinaryNode buffCheckRandomNode;
    public ActionNode buffCheckNode;
    public ActionNode healthCheckNode;
    public ActionNode attackCheckNode;
    public Sequence buffCheckSequence;
    public Selector rootNode;
```

We start off with some declarations as usual. Most notably, we declare our nodes here. We have some familiar nodes, the ActionNode, the Sequence, and the Selector, which you should be familiar with by now. But you may have also noticed an unfamiliar node as well—the RandomBinaryNode. Before digging deeper into the EnemyBehaviorTree.cs code, let's take a look at the RandomBinaryNode.cs file to see what this node type does:

```
using UnityEngine;

public class RandomBinaryNode : Node {
    public override NodeStates Evaluate() {
        var roll = Random.Range(0, 2);
        return (roll == 0 ? NodeStates.SUCCESS : NodeStates.FAILURE);
    }
}
```

As you can see, the node is very simple. We "roll" a random value between 0 and 1 (keeping in mind that Random.Range(int, int) has an exclusive upper range, meaning it can return up to that value, but not including it), and return a SUCCESS state when the roll is 0, and FAILURE otherwise.

Going back to the `EnemyBehaviorTree.cs` class, we have another delegate/event declaration:

```
public delegate void TreeExecuted();
public event TreeExecuted onTreeExecuted;
```

Similar to the `onActionExecuted` event on the `PlayerController.cs` class, this one will be called after the AI executes its action and triggers the end-of-turn checks. Up next, we have the `Start()` method, which is important as it sets up our node structure, starting from the lowest-level nodes:

```
void Start () {
    healthCheckNode = new ActionNode(CriticalHealthCheck);

    attackCheckNode = new ActionNode(CheckPlayerHealth);

    buffCheckRandomNode = new RandomBinaryNode();
    buffCheckNode = new ActionNode(BuffCheck);
    buffCheckSequence = new Sequence(new List<Node> {
        buffCheckRandomNode,
        buffCheckNode,
    });

    rootNode = new Selector(new List<Node> {
        healthCheckNode,
        attackCheckNode,
        buffCheckSequence,
    });
}
```

To better understand what's going on in this section of the code, let's take a look at the following diagram:

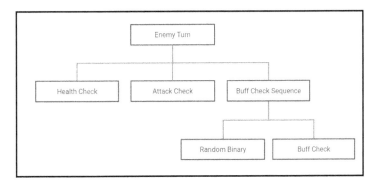

Enemy turn behavior tree

As you can see, the enemy turn is broken up into three steps—health check, attack check, and buff check. The health check node is a simple ActionNode. In this case, we're modeling a fairly conservative agent, so it prioritizes its own health versus being aggressive. The node invokes the following method:

```
private NodeStates CriticalHealthCheck() {
    if(ownData.HasLowHealth) {
        return NodeStates.SUCCESS;
    } else {
        return NodeStates.FAILURE;
    }
}
```

We then have the attack check node, which is also an ActionNode. This one then checks if the human player's health is low, and attacks if so, in an attempt to go for the kill. This is the function it invokes:

```
private NodeStates CheckPlayerHealth() {
    if(playerData.HasLowHealth) {
        return NodeStates.SUCCESS;
    } else {
        return NodeStates.FAILURE;
    }
}
```

We then have a buff check node, that is actually a sequence, with two children nodes. The idea here is that if it did not heal, and it did not attack, the agent will attempt to buff itself. However, because this would lead to a loop where it buffs itself, the player attacks (thus removing the buff), and it buffs itself over and over until its health is low, we add a randomization factor via the RandomBinaryNode node. The actual buff check calls the following method:

```
private NodeStates BuffCheck() {
    if(!ownData.IsBuffed) {
        return NodeStates.SUCCESS;
    } else {
        return NodeStates.FAILURE;
    }
}
```

The root node itself is a `Selector`, so that it only requires one child to return `SUCCESS` for it to return `SUCCESS` itself. However, we do not use the root node's state value in this example. The last part of our AI code is the `Execute()` method, which as you may notice, is a coroutine. We do this to give the illusion that the AI is "thinking" about its move. The code looks like this:

```
private IEnumerator Execute() {
    Debug.Log("The AI is thinking...");
    yield return new WaitForSeconds(2.5f);

    if(healthCheckNode.nodeState == NodeStates.SUCCESS) {
        Debug.Log("The AI decided to heal itself");
        ownData.Heal();
    } else if(attackCheckNode.nodeState == NodeStates.SUCCESS) {
        Debug.Log("The AI decided to attack the player!");
        playerData.Damage();
    } else if (buffCheckSequence.nodeState == NodeStates.SUCCESS) {
        Debug.Log("The AI decided to defend itself");
        ownData.Buff();
    } else {
        Debug.Log("The AI finally decided to attack the player");
        playerData.Damage();
    }
    if(onTreeExecuted != null) {
        onTreeExecuted();
    }
}
```

We evaluate the state of each node, and act accordingly. In the case that all nodes report a `FAILURE`, we fall back to an `else` clause that attacks the enemy. At each stage we debug the AI's "process" via debug logs. After all the `if` checks, we simply fire off our callback, which in turn calls the `EndTurn()` method we passed in earlier via the `Game.cs` script.

The last bit of code to look at for this example is the `EnemyTurnState.cs` `StateMachineBehaviour` script. It's attached to the **Enemy Turn** state in the state machine. In it, we only implement the following two methods:

```
override public void OnStateEnter(Animator animator, AnimatorStateInfo
stateInfo, int layerIndex) {
    Debug.Log("******************** \n Strating the enemy's turn!");
    animator.gameObject.GetComponent<Game>().EvaluateAITree();
}
```

As you can see, `OnStateEnter` logs some information to the console, then calls the `EvaluteAITree()` method on the `Game.cs` script, which in turn calls the `Evaluate()` method on the `EnemyBehaviorTree.cs` script:

```
override public void OnStateExit(Animator animator, AnimatorStateInfo
stateInfo, int layerIndex) {
    Debug.Log("Ending the enemy's turn. \n *********************");
}
```

The `OnStateExit` method simply logs out some information to the console, so that when we enter play mode in the editor, we'll see an output that looks like the following screenshot:

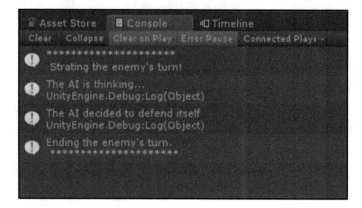

The preceding screenshot shows the console after the AI's first turn, where neither the AI agent nor the player have sustained enough damage for them to heal or attack, and the AI opted to defend itself instead, using the **Buff** ability.

Testing the game

All you have to do is hit play, and play along. Each game should play differently depending on how the randomness of the abilities and the `RandomBinaryNode` play out. As you can see, even with the simple three-branch behavior tree used here, we're able to create a huge number of possible outcomes for the game. Adding more branches to suit your game design can give your game added challenge, replay value, and unpredictability.

Summary

In this chapter, we dug into how a behavior tree works, and then we looked at each individual type of node that can make up a behavior tree. We also learned the different scenarios where some nodes would be more helpful than others. After looking at some off-the-shelf solutions available in the Unity asset store, we applied this knowledge by implementing our own basic behavior tree framework in C# and explored its inner workings. With the knowledge and the tools out of the way, we created a sample behavior tree using our framework to test the concepts learned throughout the chapter. We then went on to explore the implementation of *HomeRock*, a sample card game that showcases an AI opponent. This knowledge prepares us to harness the power of behavior trees in games and take our AI implementations to the next level.

In the next chapter, Chapter 7, *Using Fuzzy Logic to Make Your AI Seem Alive*, we'll look at new ways to add complexity and functionality to the concepts we've learned in this chapter, modifying behavior trees and FSMs, which we covered in Chapter 2, *Finite State Machines and You*, via the concept of fuzzy logic.

7

Using Fuzzy Logic to Make Your AI Seem Alive

Fuzzy logic is a fantastic way to represent the rules of your game in a more nuanced way. Perhaps more so than other concepts in this book, fuzzy logic is a very math-heavy topic. Most of the information can be represented purely in mathematical functions. For the sake of teaching the important concepts as they apply to Unity, most of the math has been simplified and implemented using Unity's built-in features. Of course, if you are the type who loves math, this is a somewhat deep topic in that regard, so feel free to take the concepts covered in this book and run with them! In this chapter, we'll learn the following:

- What fuzzy logic is
- Where fuzzy logic is used
- How to implement fuzzy logic controllers
- What the other creative uses for fuzzy logic concepts are

Technical Requirements

You will be required to have Unity 2017 installed on a system that has either Windows 7 SP1+, 8, 10, 64-bit versions or Mac OS X 10.9+. The code in this book will not run on Windows XP and Vista, and server versions of Windows and OS X are not tested.

The code files of this chapter can be found on GitHub:
`https://github.com/PacktPublishing/Unity-2017-Game-AI-Programming-Third-Edition/tree/master/Chapter07`

Check out the following video to see the code in action:
`https://goo.gl/KqRDTy`

Defining fuzzy logic

The simplest way to define fuzzy logic is by comparison to binary logic. In the previous chapters, we looked at transition rules as true or false or 0 or 1 values. Is something visible? Is it at least a certain distance away? Even in instances where multiple values were being evaluated, all of the values had exactly two outcomes; thus, they were binary. In contrast, fuzzy values represent a much richer range of possibilities, where each value is represented as a float rather than an integer. We stop looking at values as 0 or 1, and we start looking at them as 0 to 1.

A common example used to describe fuzzy logic is temperature. Fuzzy logic allows us to make decisions based on non-specific data. I can step outside on a sunny Californian summer's day and ascertain that it is warm, without knowing the temperature precisely. Conversely, if I were to find myself in Alaska during the winter, I would know that it is cold, again, without knowing the exact temperature. These concepts of cold, cool, warm, and hot are fuzzy ones. There is a good amount of ambiguity as to at what point we go from warm to hot. Fuzzy logic allows us to model these concepts as sets and determine their validity or truth by using a set of rules.

When people make decisions, people have some gray areas. That is to say, it's not always black and white. The same concept applies to agents that rely on fuzzy logic. Say you hadn't eaten in a few hours, and you were starting to feel a little hungry. At which point were you hungry enough to go grab a snack? You could look at the time right after a meal as 0, and 1 would be the point where you approached starvation. The following figure illustrates this point:

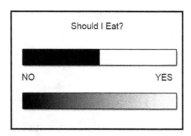

When making decisions, there are many factors that determine the ultimate choice. This leads into another aspect of fuzzy logic controllers—they can take into account as much data as necessary. Let's continue to look at our "should I eat?" example. We've only considered one value for making that decision, which is the time since the last time you ate. However, there are other factors that can affect this decision, such as how much energy you're expending and how lazy you are at that particular moment. Or am I the only one to use that as a deciding factor? Either way, you can see how multiple input values can affect the output, which we can think of as the "likeliness to have another meal."

Fuzzy logic systems can be very flexible due to their generic nature. You provide input, the fuzzy logic provides an output. What that output means to your game is entirely up to you. We've primarily looked at how the inputs would affect a decision, which, in reality, is taking the output and using it in a way the computer, our agent, can understand. However, the output can also be used to determine how much of something to do, how fast something happens, or for how long something happens.

For example, imagine your agent is a car in a sci-fi racing game that has a "nitro-boost" ability that lets it expend a resource to go faster. Our 0 to 1 value can represent a normalized amount of time for it to use that boost or perhaps a normalized amount of fuel to use.

Picking fuzzy systems over binary systems

As with the previous systems we covered in this book, and with most things in game programming, we must evaluate the requirements of our game and the technology and hardware limitations when deciding on the best way to tackle a problem.

As you might imagine, there is a performance cost associated with going from a simple yes/no system to a more nuanced fuzzy logic one, which is one of the reasons we may opt out of using it. Of course, being a more complex system doesn't necessarily always mean it's a better one. There will be times when you just want the simplicity and predictability of a binary system because it may fit your game better.

While there is some truth to the old adage, "the simpler, the better", one should also take into account the saying, "everything should be made as simple as possible, but not simpler". Though the quote is widely attributed to Albert Einstein, the father of relativity, it's not entirely clear who said it. The important thing to consider is the meaning of the quote itself. You should make your AI as simple as your game needs it to be, but not simpler. Pac-Man's AI works perfectly for the game–it's simple enough. However, rules say that simple would be out of place in a modern shooter or strategy game.

Take the knowledge and examples in this book and find what works best for you.

Using fuzzy logic

Once you understand the simple concepts behind fuzzy logic, it's easy to start thinking of the many, many ways in which it can be useful. In reality, it's just another tool in our belt, and each job requires different tools.

Fuzzy logic is great at taking some data, evaluating it in a similar way to how a human would (albeit in a much simpler way), and then translating the data back to information that is usable by the system.

Fuzzy logic controllers have several real-world use cases. Some are more obvious than others, and while these are by no means one-to-one comparisons to our usage in game AI, they serve to illustrate a point:

- **Heating ventilation and air conditioning (HVAC) systems**: The temperature example when talking about fuzzy logic is not only a good theoretical approach to explaining fuzzy logic, but also a very common real-world example of fuzzy logic controllers in action.
- **Automobiles**: Modern automobiles come equipped with very sophisticated computerized systems, from the air conditioning system (again), to fuel delivery, to automated braking systems. In fact, putting computers in automobiles has resulted in far more efficient systems than the old binary systems that were sometimes used.
- **Your smartphone**: Ever notice how your screen dims and brightens depending on how much ambient light there is? Modern smartphone operating systems look at ambient light, the color of the data being displayed, and the current battery life to optimize screen brightness.
- **Washing machines**: Not my washing machine necessarily, as it's quite old, but most modern washers (from the last 20 years) make some use of fuzzy logic. Load size, water dirtiness, temperature, and other factors are taken into account from cycle to cycle to optimize water use, energy consumption, and time.

If you take a look around your house, there is a good chance you'll find a few interesting uses of fuzzy logic, and I mean besides your computer, of course. While these are neat uses of the concept, they're not particularly exciting or game-related. I'm partial to games involving wizards, magic, and monsters, so let's look at a more relevant example.

Implementing a simple fuzzy logic system

For this example, we're going to use my good friend, Bob, the wizard. Bob lives in an RPG world, and he has some very powerful healing magic at his disposal. Bob has to decide when to cast this magic on himself based on his remaining **health points** (**HPs**).

In a binary system, Bob's decision-making process might look like this:

```
if(healthPoints <= 50)
{
  CastHealingSpell(me);
}
```

We see that Bob's health can be in one of two states—above 50, or not. Nothing wrong with that, but let's have a look at what the fuzzy version of this same scenario might look like, starting with determining Bob's health status:

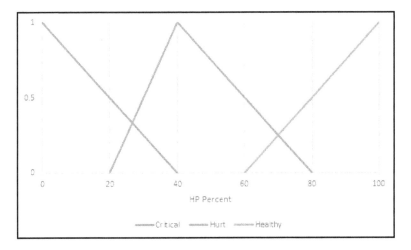

A typical function representing fuzzy values

Before the panic sets in upon seeing charts and values that may not quite mean anything to you right away, let's dissect what we're looking at. Our first impulse might be to try to map the probability that Bob will cast a healing spell to how much health he is missing. That would, in simple terms, just be a linear function. Nothing really fuzzy about that—it's a linear relationship, and while it is a step above a binary decision in terms of complexity, it's still not truly fuzzy.

Enter the concept of a membership function. It's key to our system, as it allows us to determine how true a statement is. In this example, we're not simply looking at raw values to determine whether or not Bob should cast his spell; instead, we're breaking it up into logical chunks of information for Bob to use in order to determine what his course of action should be.

In this example, we're comparing three statements and evaluating not only how true each one is, but which is the most true:

- Bob is in a critical condition
- Bob is hurt
- Bob is healthy

If you're into official terminology, we call this determining the degree of membership to a set. Once we have this information, our agent can determine what to do with it next.

At a glance, you'll notice it's possible for two statements to be true at a time. Bob can be in a critical condition and hurt. He can also be somewhat hurt and a little bit healthy. You're free to pick the thresholds for each, but, in this example, let's evaluate these statements as per the preceding graph. The vertical value represents the degree of truth of a statement as a normalized float (0 to 1):

- At 0 percent health, we can see that the critical statement evaluates to 1. It is absolutely true that Bob is critical when his health is gone.
- At 40 percent health, Bob is hurt, and that is the truest statement.
- At 100 percent health, the truest statement is that Bob is healthy.

Anything outside of these absolutely true statements is squarely in fuzzy territory. For example, let's say Bob's health is at 65 percent. In that same chart, we can visualize it like this:

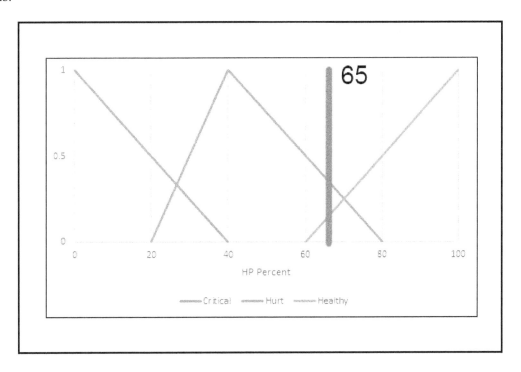

Bob's health at 65 percent

The vertical line drawn through the chart at **65** represents Bob's health. As we can see, it intersects both sets, which means that Bob is a little bit hurt, but he's also kind of healthy. At a glance, we can tell, however, that the vertical line intercepts the **Hurt** set at a higher point in the graph. We can take this to mean that Bob is more hurt than he is healthy. To be specific, Bob is 37.5 percent hurt, 12.5 percent healthy, and 0 percent critical. Let's take a look at this in code; open up our `FuzzySample` scene in Unity. The hierarchy will look like this:

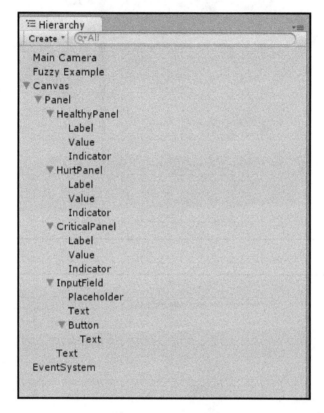

The hierarchy setup in our sample scene

The important game object to look at is `Fuzzy Example`. This contains the logic that we'll be looking at. In addition to that, we have our `Canvas` containing all of the labels and the input field and button that make this example work. Lastly, there's the Unity-generated `EventSystem` and `Main Camera`, which we can disregard. There isn't anything special going on with the setup for the scene, but it's a good idea to become familiar with it, and you are encouraged to poke around and tweak it to your heart's content after we've looked at why everything is there and what it all does.

With the `Fuzzy Example` game object selected, the inspector will look similar to the following image:

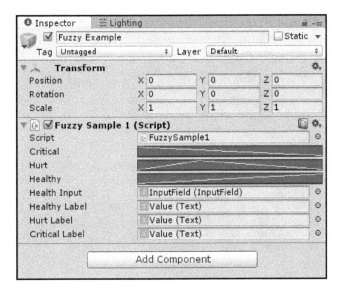

The Fuzzy Example game object inspector

Our sample implementation is not necessarily something you'll take and implement in your game as it is, but it is meant to illustrate the previous points in a clear manner. We use Unity's `AnimationCurve` for each different set. It's a quick and easy way to visualize the very same lines in our earlier graph.

Unfortunately, there is no straightforward way to plot all the lines in the same graph, so we use a separate `AnimationCurve` for each set. In the preceding screenshot, they are labeled **Critical**, **Hurt**, and **Healthy**. The neat thing about these curves is that they come with a built-in method to evaluate them at a given point (*t*). For us, *t* does not represent time, but rather the amount of health Bob has.

As in the preceding graph, the Unity example looks at a HP range of 0 to 100. These curves also provide a simple user interface for editing the values. You can simply click on the curve in the inspector. That opens up the curve editing window. You can add points, move points, change tangents, and so on, as shown in the following screenshot:

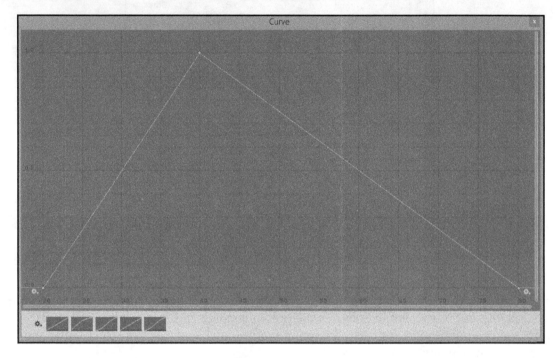

Unity's curve editor window

Our example focuses on triangle-shaped sets. That is, linear graphs for each set. You are by no means restricted to this shape, though it is the most common. You could use a bell curve or a trapezoid, for that matter. To keep things simple, we'll stick to the triangle.

 You can learn more about Unity's `AnimationCurve` editor at
`http://docs.unity3d.com/ScriptReference/AnimationCurve.html`.

The rest of the fields are just references to the different UI elements used in code that we'll be looking at later in this chapter. The names of these variables are fairly self-explanatory, however, so there isn't much guesswork to be done here.

Next, we can take a look at how the scene is set up. If you play the scene, the game view will look something similar to the following screenshot:

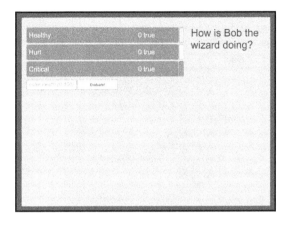

A simple UI to demonstrate fuzzy values

We can see that we have three distinct groups, representing each question from the "Bob, the wizard" example. How healthy is Bob, how hurt is Bob, and how critical is Bob? For each set, upon evaluation, the value that starts off as **0 true** will dynamically adjust to represent the actual degree of membership.

There is an input box in which you can type a percentage of health to use for the test. No fancy controls are in place for this, so be sure to enter a value from 0 to 100. For the sake of consistency, let's enter a value of 65 into the box and then press the **Evaluate!** button.

This will run some code, look at the curves, and yield the exact same results we saw in our graph earlier. While this shouldn't come as a surprise (the math is what it is, after all), there are fewer things more important in game programming than testing your assumptions, and sure enough, we've tested and verified our earlier statement.

After running the test by hitting the **Evaluate!** button, the game scene will look similar to the following screenshot:

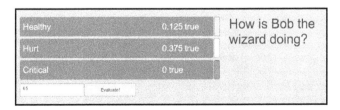

This is how Bob is doing at 65 percent health

Again, the values turn out to be 0.125 (or 12.5 percent) healthy and 0.375 (or 37.5 percent) hurt. At this point, we're still not doing anything with this data, but let's take a look at the code that's handling everything:

```
using UnityEngine;
using UnityEngine.UI;
using System.Collections;

public class FuzzySample1 : MonoBehaviour {
    private const string labelText = "{0} true";
    public AnimationCurve critical;
    public AnimationCurve hurt;
    public AnimationCurve healthy;

    public InputField healthInput;

    public Text healthyLabel;
    public Text hurtLabel;
    public Text criticalLabel;

    private float criticalValue = 0f;
    private float hurtValue = 0f;
    private float healthyValue = 0f;
```

We start off by declaring some variables. The `labelText` is simply a constant we use to plug into our label. We replace `{0}` with the real value.

Next, we declare the three `AnimationCurve` variables that we mentioned earlier. Making these public or otherwise accessible from the inspector is key to being able to edit them visually (though it is possible to construct curves by code), which is the whole point of using them.

The following four variables are just references to UI elements that we saw earlier in the screenshot of our inspector, and the last three variables are the actual float values that our curves will evaluate into:

```
    private void Start () {
        SetLabels();
    }

    /*
     * Evaluates all the curves and returns float values
     */
    public void EvaluateStatements() {
        if (string.IsNullOrEmpty(healthInput.text)) {
            return;
```

```
    }
    float inputValue = float.Parse(healthInput.text);
    healthyValue = healthy.Evaluate(inputValue);
    hurtValue = hurt.Evaluate(inputValue);
    criticalValue = critical.Evaluate(inputValue);

    SetLabels();
}
```

The `Start()` method doesn't require much explanation. We simply update our labels here so that they initialize to something other than the default text. The `EvaluateStatements()` method is much more interesting. We first do some simple null checking for our input string. We don't want to try and parse an empty string, so we return out of the function if it is empty. As mentioned earlier, there is no check in place to validate that you've input a numerical value, so be sure not to accidentally input a non-numerical value or you'll get an error.

For each of the `AnimationCurve` variables, we call the `Evaluate(float t)` method, where we replace `t` with the parsed value we get from the input field. In the example we ran, that value would be 65. Then, we update our labels once again to display the values we got. The code looks similar to this:

```
/*
 * Updates the GUI with the evluated values based
 * on the health percentage entered by the
 * user.
 */
private void SetLabels() {
    healthyLabel.text = string.Format(labelText, healthyValue);
    hurtLabel.text = string.Format(labelText, hurtValue);
    criticalLabel.text = string.Format(labelText, criticalValue);
}
}
```

We simply take each label and replace the text with a formatted version of our `labelText` constant that replaces the `{0}` with the real value.

Expanding the sets

We discussed this topic in detail earlier, and it's important to understand that the values that make up the sets in our example are unique to Bob and his pain threshold. Let's say we have a second wizard, Jim, who's a bit more reckless. For him, critical might be below 20 percent, rather than 40 percent as it is for Bob. This is what I like to call a "happy bonus" from using fuzzy logic. Each agent in the game can have different rules that define their sets, but the system doesn't care. You could predefine these rules or have some degree of randomness determine the limits, and every single agent would behave uniquely and respond to things in their own way.

In addition, there is no reason to limit our sets to just three. Why not four or five? To the fuzzy logic controller, all that matters is that you determine what truth you're trying to arrive at, and how you get there; it doesn't care how many different sets or possibilities exist in that system.

Defuzzifying the data

Yes, that's a real (sort of) word. We've started with some crisp rules, which, in the context of fuzzy logic, means clear-cut, hard-defined data, which we then fuzzified (again, a sort of real word) by assigning membership functions to sets. The last step of the process is to defuzzify the data and make a decision. For this, we use simple Boolean operations, such as the following:

```
IF health IS critical THEN cast healing spell
```

Now, at this point, you may be saying, "Hold on a second. That looks an awful lot like a binary controller," and you'd be correct. So why go through all the trouble? Remember what we said earlier about ambiguous information? Without a fuzzy controller, how does our agent understand what it means to be critical, hurt, or healthy, for that matter? These are abstract concepts that mean very little on their own to a computer.

By using fuzzy logic, we're now able to use these vague terms, infer something from them, and do concrete things; in this case, cast a healing spell. Furthermore, we're able to allow each agent to determine what these vague terms mean to them on an individual level, allowing us not only to achieve unpredictability on an individual level, but even amongst several similar agents.

The process is described best in the following diagram:

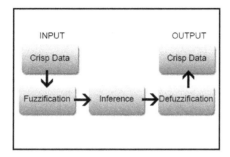

The fuzzy logic controller flow

At the end of the day, they are still computers, so we're bound to the most basic thing computers understand, 0s and 1s:

- We start with crisp data, that is, concrete, hard values that tell us something very specific.
- The fuzzification step is where we get to decide the abstract or ambiguous data that our agent will need to make a decision.
- During the inference step, our agent gets to decide what that data means. The agent gets to determine what is "true" based on a provided set of rules, meant to mimic the nuance of human decision-making.
- The defuzzification step takes this human-friendly data and converts it into simple, computer-friendly information.
- We end with crisp data, ready for our wizard agent to use.

Using the resulting crisp data

The data output from a fuzzy controller can then be plugged into a behavior tree or a finite state machine. Of course, we can also combine multiple controllers' output to make decisions. In fact, we can take a whole bunch of them to achieve the most realistic or interesting result (as realistic as a magic-using wizard can be, anyway).

The following figure illustrates a potential set of fuzzy logic controllers it can be used to determine whether or not to cast the heal spell:

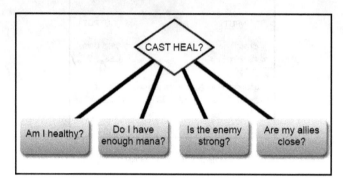

We've looked at the health question already, but what about the rest? We have another set of questions that really don't mean much to our agent on their own:

Do you have enough mana? Well, you can have a little bit of mana, some mana, or a lot of mana. It would not be uncommon for a human player to ask this question as they choose to cast a magic spell in a game or use an ability. "Enough" may literally be a binary amount, but more likely, it would be "enough to cast heal, and have some left for other spells." We start with a straightforward crisp value–the amount of mana the agent has available that we then stick to our fuzzy logic controller and get some crisp data at the other end.

What about the enemy's strength? He could be weak, average, strong, or unbeatable. You can get creative with the input for your fuzzy logic controllers. You could, for example, just take a raw "strength" value from your enemy, but you could also take the difference between your "defensive" stat and the enemy's "attack power," and plug that into your fuzzy logic controller. Remember, there is no restriction on how you process the data before it goes into the controller.

Are my allies close? As we saw in Chapter 2, *Finite State Machines and You*, a simple distance check can do wonders for a simple design, but, at times, you may need more than just that. You may need to take into account obstacles along the way—is that an ally behind a locked gate, making him unable to reach the agent? These types of questions could even be a nested set of statements that we need to evaluate.

Now, if we were to take that last question with the nested controllers, it might start to look a little familiar:

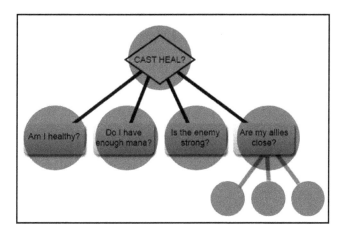

The preceding figure is quite tree-like, isn't it? Sure enough, there is no reason why you couldn't build a behavior tree using fuzzy logic to evaluate each node. We end up with a very flexible, powerful, and nuanced AI system by combining these two concepts.

Using a simpler approach

If you choose to stick with a simple evaluation of the crisp output, in other words, not specifically a tree or an FSM, you can use more Boolean operators to decide what your agent is going to do. The pseudo code would look like this:

```
IF health IS critical AND mana IS plenty THEN cast heal
```

We can check for conditions that are not true:

```
IF health IS critical AND allies ARE NOT close THEN cast heal
```

We can also string multiple conditions together:

```
IF health IS critical AND mana IS NOT depleted AND enemy IS very strong
THEN cast heal
```

By looking at these simplified statements, you will have noticed yet another "happy bonus" of using fuzzy logic—the crisp output abstracts much of the decision-making conditionals and combines them into simplified data.

Rather than having to parse through all the possibilities in your `if/else` statements and ending up with a bazillion of them or a gazillion switch statements, you can neatly bundle pockets of logic into fewer, more meaningful chunks of data.

In other words, you don't have to nest all the statements in a procedural way that is hard to read and difficult to reuse. As a design pattern, abstracting data via a fuzzy logic controller ends up being much more object-oriented and friendlier.

The morality meter example

The faction/morality meter example for this chapter covers a slightly different approach to implementing fuzzy logic via Unity. We build upon the implementation we covered in the basic fuzzy logic example.

In this example, we create a simple dialogue sequence, where the player is presented a series of scenarios, or questions, that they can then answer according to their morality. For simplicity's sake, we've included a "good," "neutral," and "evil" answer for each question. Let's take a look at the code to understand this a bit better.

The question and answer classes

The `Question` and `Answer` classes are very simple, and are used as data containers. Let's look at the `Question.cs` class first:

```
[System.Serializable]
public class Question {
    public string questionText;
    public Answer[] answers;
}
```

You may have noticed that the `Question` class does not derive from `MonoBehaviour`. It is a plain ol' vanilla C# class. As such, Unity will not serialize it by default, and it won't show up in the inspector. To let Unity know you want this class to be serialized, use the `System.Serializable` attribute at the top of the class definition.

As you can see, it's only a few lines of code. The first field, `questionText`, will be edited via the inspector in a later step. It is the display text for the question/scenario we are presenting the user. The `answers` field is an array of `Answer` types. The `Answer.cs` code looks like this:

```
[System.Serializable]
public class Answer {
    public string answerText;
    public float moralityValue;
}
```

Again, you'll notice this class is very simple. `answerText` is the text to display in the response button for the player, and the `moralityValue` field is a hidden value we use to calculate the player's morality alignment later on. For this example, we assume that each question has three answers and that the morality values are 0, 50, and 100 for each one.

Managing the conversation

Our `ConversationManager.cs` class is where all the heavy lifting happens for this sample. It manages the UI for our conversation, handles events, and calculates the results for us. For the first part, we initialize our question array and then handle the UI. We set up some variables at the top of the class, which looks like this:

```
[Header("UI")]
[SerializeField]
private GameObject questionPanel;
[SerializeField]
private GameObject resultPanel;
[SerializeField]
private Text resultText;
[SerializeField]
private Text questionText;
[SerializeField]
private Button firstAnswerButton;
[SerializeField]
private Button secondAnswerButton;
[SerializeField]
private Button thirdAnswerButton;
```

We'll be able to see the UI elements these variables correspond to up ahead, but note that we explicitly expect a set number of answers, as we only provide three answer buttons for the UI. Of course, you can modify this to be more flexible or to fit your needs, but keep in mind that if you want to use more or fewer answers, you'll need to make those changes here as well:

```
[Header("Morality Gradient")]
[SerializeField]
private AnimationCurve good;
[SerializeField]
private AnimationCurve neutral;
[SerializeField]
private AnimationCurve evil;
```

Similar to our previous example, we use Unity's `AnimationCurve` to specify our fuzzy values. We assume a few things with this setup:

- At *t=0*, our "good" value is at 1, and goes down to 0 from there
- At *t=50*, our "neutral" value is at 1
- At *t=100*, our "evil" rating is at 1

These values can be tweaked to your liking, but the current setup works well for the example. The following screenshot shows the curves set in the inspector:

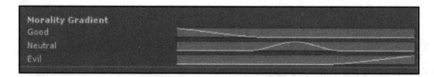

Fuzzy curves for our morality gradient

Notice that the values shown here correspond to our earlier assumption that our "good" answer gives a value of 0, our "neutral" answer has a value of 50, and our "evil" answer has a value of 100.

Loading up the questions

We provide a simple method named `LoadQuestion` to pull the values from our data classes into the UI and display them to the player. The code looks like this:

```
private void LoadQuestion(int index)
{
    if (index < questions.Length)
    {
        questionText.text = questions[index].questionText;
        firstAnswerButton.GetComponentInChildren<Text>().text =
questions[index].answers[0].answerText;
        secondAnswerButton.GetComponentInChildren<Text>().text =
questions[index].answers[1].answerText;
        thirdAnswerButton.GetComponentInChildren<Text>().text =
questions[index].answers[2].answerText;
    }
    else
    {
        EndConversation();
    }
}
```

The `LoadQuestion` method takes in a question index, which corresponds to the index of the question in the array `questions[]`. We first check that our index is in bounds, and end the conversation by calling `EndConversation()` if it isn't. If we are in bounds, we just populate the question text and the answer text for each answer button.

Handling user input

The event that gets called when the user presses an answer button on the UI is `OnAnswerSubmitted`. The method is quite simple and is only a few lines of code:

```
public void OnAnswerSubmitted(int answerIndex)
{
    answerTotal +=
questions[questionIndex].answers[answerIndex].moralityValue;
    questionIndex++;
    LoadQuestion(questionIndex);
}
```

The method does a few things:

- It aggregates the answer value to the answer total. We'll look at how these values are assigned up ahead.
- It increments the question index value.
- Finally, it calls `LoadQuestion` with the incremented index value from the previous bullet.

Calculating the results

Finally, we have the `EndConversation` method, which, as we saw, gets called when we have answered all the questions (and the question index is out of bounds, based on our `questions[]` array length).

The first line simply disables the panel game object containing the question UI:

```
questionPanel.SetActive(false);
```

The calculations are in the next block of code:

```
float average = answerTotal / questions.Length;
float goodRating = good.Evaluate(average);
float neutralRating = neutral.Evaluate(average);
float evilRating = evil.Evaluate(average);
```

We calculate the average of all of our answers by taking the `answerTotal` value (the sum of all the answers) and dividing it by the number of questions. We then individually evaluate each curve for good, neutral, and evil ratings using the average value we just calculated. We use the average as our *t* value in the evaluation method.

Next, we use some simple `if` logic to determine which rating is higher, as seen in the following snippet:

```
if(goodRating > neutralRating)
    {
        if(goodRating > evilRating)
        {
            //good wins
            alignmentText = "GOOD";
        }
        else
        {
            //evil wins
            alignmentText = "EVIL";
```

```
        }
    }
    else
    {
        if(neutralRating > evilRating)
        {
            //neutral wins
            alignmentText = "NEUTRAL";
        }
        else
        {
            //evil win
            alignmentText = "EVIL";
        }
    }
```

As you can see in the previous code, we have a little bit of a branching conditional structure to determine the highest value, from which we set the `alignmentText` value accordingly.

> `if` blocks can get a bit complex if you start to add too many conditions. In this case, you may want to consider placing the ratings into an array or dictionary, then sorting them, and/or using LINQ to get the highest value from it. For more on sorting dictionaries, check out Dot Net Perls: `https://www.dotnetperls.com/sort-dictionary`

Lastly, we display the results to the user:

```
resultPanel.SetActive(true);
resultText.text = "Your morality alignment is: " + alignmentText;
```

We simply enable the results panel, and then append `alignmentText` to the `"Your morality alignment is:"` message, which would look like this in play mode (if you have a "good" rating):

The game screen when you earn a "good" rating

Next up, we can take a look at our scene setup, and how all of our values get initialized for the sample project.

Scene setup

When you first open the `FactionScene` example scene, you'll notice a UI that looks like this screenshot:

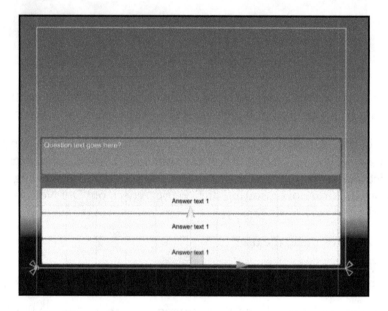

The sample scene UI setup

As you can see in the preceding screenshot, the UI comprises several different panels, and the text components have been initialized with some sample text to help organize everything nicely. The hierarchy for the scene is shown in this screenshot:

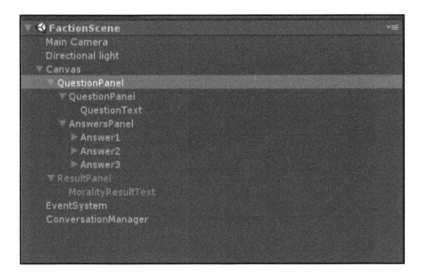

The FactionScene hierarchy

As you can see, our canvas has two main panels at the root level—the **QuestionPanel** and a **ResultPanel**, which is disabled by default. This is because, as you may remember, we set that panel to `enabled` via code in our `EndConversation` method. At the bottom of the list, we have our **ConversationManager** game object, which contains our `ConversationManager` script.

If you select it, you'll see that the inspector looks like this:

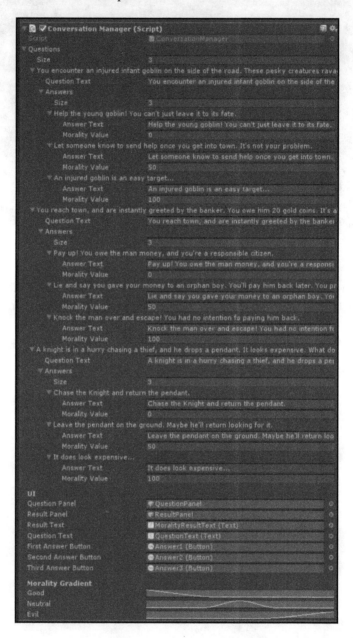

The inspector for our Conversation Manager with all the values assigned

At first glance, the amount of information here may seem daunting, but let's take a look at each step, and you'll realize we've covered all of this already.

We first have our serialized array of questions. In this case, we have three questions (feel free to add more!). Each question then contains an array of (exactly) three answers, and the question text we saw earlier. For each answer, we have the answer text and morality value we saw earlier as well. Note that the order of the questions or answers doesn't necessarily matter, so long as your morality value corresponds to good, neutral, or evil.

We then have the UI section, in which we assign all the necessary elements. Everything in the hierarchy is named appropriately to make it easy to ensure that each field is populated with the correct game object.

Lastly, we have the morality curves that we saw previously. Again, feel free to tweak these to your heart's content!

Testing the example

All that's left is to test the example! Hit play, and select some answers. The scenario provided puts you in the shoes of an adventurer heading into town. On his way, he encounters a goblin, a banker, and a knight. What would you do in each scenario? Feel free to play around with the wording, and add your own moral dilemmas!

Finding other uses for fuzzy logic

Fuzzy data is very peculiar and interesting in that it can be used in tandem with all of the major concepts we have introduced in this book. We saw how a series of fuzzy logic controllers can easily fit into a behavior tree structure, and it's not terribly difficult to imagine how it could be used with an FSM.

Merging with other concepts

Sensory systems also tend to make use of fuzzy logic. While seeing something can be a binary condition, in low-light or low-contrast environments, we can suddenly see how fuzzy the condition can become. You've probably experienced it at night: seeing an odd shape, dark in the distance, in the shadows, thinking "is that a cat?". It then turns out to be a trash bag, some other animal, or perhaps even your imagination. The same can be applied to sounds and smells.

When it comes to pathfinding, we run into the cost of traversing certain areas of a grid, which a fuzzy logic controller can easily help to fuzzify and make more interesting.

Should Bob cross the bridge and fight his way through the guards, or risk crossing the river and fighting the current? Well, if he's a good swimmer and a poor fighter, the choice is clear, right?

Creating a truly unique experience

Our agents can use fuzzy logic to mimic personalities. Some agents may be more "brave" than others. Suddenly, their personal characteristics—how fast they are, how far they can run, their size, and so on—can be leveraged to arrive at the decisions that are unique to that agent.

Personalities can be applied to enemies, allies and friends, NPCs, or even to the rules of the game. The game can take in crisp data from the player's progress, style of play, or level of progression, and dynamically adjust the difficulty to provide a more unique and personalized challenge.

Fuzzy logic can even be used to dole out the technical game rules, such as the number of players in a given multiplayer lobby, the type of data to display to the player, and even how players are matched against other players. Taking the player's statistics and plugging those into a matchmaking system can help keep the player engaged by pitting them against the players that either match their style of play in a cooperative environment or players of a similar skill level in a competitive environment.

Summary

I'm glad to see that you've made it to the end of the chapter. Fuzzy logic tends to become far less fuzzy once you understand the basic concepts. Being one of the more pure math concepts in the book, it can be a little daunting if you're not familiar with the lingo, but when presented in a familiar context, the mystery fades away, and you're left with a very powerful tool to use in your game.

We learned how fuzzy logic is used in the real world, and how it can help illustrate vague concepts in a way that binary systems cannot. We also learned how to implement our own fuzzy logic controllers using the concepts of member functions, degrees of membership, and fuzzy sets. In addition to this, we also played around with a faction/morality system to further illustrate the concept of fuzzy logic in the context of a choose-your-own-adventure-style interaction. Lastly, we explored the various ways in which we can use the resulting data, and how it can help make our agents more unique.

In the final chapter, we will look at several of the concepts introduced in this book working together.

8
How It All Comes Together

We've almost arrived at the end of our journey. We've learned all the essential tools to implement fun AI in our Unity game. We stressed this throughout the course of the book, but it's important to drive the point home: the concepts and patterns we learned throughout the book are individual concepts, but they can, and often should, be used in harmony to achieve the desired behavior from our AI. Before we say our goodbyes, we'll look at a simple tank-defense game that implements some of the concepts that we've learned to achieve a cohesive "game," and I only say "game" because this is more of a blueprint for you to expand upon and play with. In this chapter, we will:

- Integrate some of the systems we've learned in a single project
- Create an AI tower agent
- Create our `NavMeshAgent` tank
- Set up the environment
- Test our sample scene

Technical Requirements

You will be required to have Unity 2017 installed on a system that has either Windows 7 SP1+, 8, 10, 64-bit versions or Mac OS X 10.9+. The code in this book will not run on Windows XP and Vista, and server versions of Windows and OS X are not tested.

The code files of this chapter can be found on GitHub:
`https://github.com/PacktPublishing/Unity-2017-Game-AI-Programming-Third-Edition/tree/master/Chapter08`

Check out the following video to see the code in action:
`https://goo.gl/JBmyyc`

Setting up the rules

Our "game" is quite simple. While the actual game logic, such as health, damage, and win conditions, are left completely up to you, our example focuses on setting you up to implement your own tank-defense game.

When deciding on what kind of logic and behavior you'll need from your agent, it's important to have the rules of the game fleshed out beyond a simple idea. Of course, as you implement different features, those rules can change, but having a set of concepts nailed down early on will help you pick the best tools for the job.

It's a bit of a twist on the traditional tower-defense genre. You don't build towers to stop an oncoming enemy; you rather use your abilities to help your tank get through a gauntlet of towers. As your tank traverses the maze, towers along the path will attempt to destroy your tank by shooting explosive projectiles at it. To help your tank get to the other side, you can use two abilities:

- **Boost**: This ability doubles your tank's movement speed for a short period of time. This is great for getting away from a projectile in a bind.
- **Shield**: This creates a shield around your tank for a short period of time to block oncoming projectiles.

For our example, we'll implement the towers using a finite state machine, since they have a limited number of states and don't require the extra complexity of a behavior tree. The towers will also need to be able to be aware of their surroundings, or more specifically, whether the tank is nearby so that they can shoot at it, so we'll use a sphere trigger to model the towers' field of vision and sensing. The tank needs to be able to navigate the environment on its own, so we use a NavMesh and `NavMeshAgent` to achieve this.

Creating the towers

In the sample project for this chapter, you'll find a `Tower` prefab in the `Prefabs` folder. The tower itself is quite simple; it's just a group of primitives arranged to look like a cannon, as you can see in the following screenshot:

Our beautiful primitive shape tower

The barrel of the gun is affixed to the spherical part of the tower. The gun can rotate freely on its axis when tracking the player so that it can fire in the direction of its target, but it is immobile in every other way. Once the tank gets far enough away, the tower cannot chase it or reposition itself.

In the sample scene, there are several towers placed throughout the level. As they are prefabbed, it's very easy to duplicate towers, move them around, and reuse them between the levels. Their setup is not terribly complicated either. Their hierarchy looks similar to the following screenshot:

The Tower hierarchy in the inspector

The breakdown of the hierarchy is as follows:

- `Tower`: Technically, this is the base of the tower: the cylinder that holds the rest of it up. This serves no function but to hold the rest of the parts.
- `Gun`: The gun is where most of the magic happens. It is the sphere mounted on the tower with the barrel on it. This is the part of the tower that moves and tracks the player.
- `Barrel` and `Muzzle`: The muzzle is located at the tip of the barrel. This is used as the spawn point for the bullets that come out of the gun.

We mentioned that the gun is where the business happens for the tower, so let's dig in a bit deeper. The inspector with the gun selected looks similar to the following screenshot:

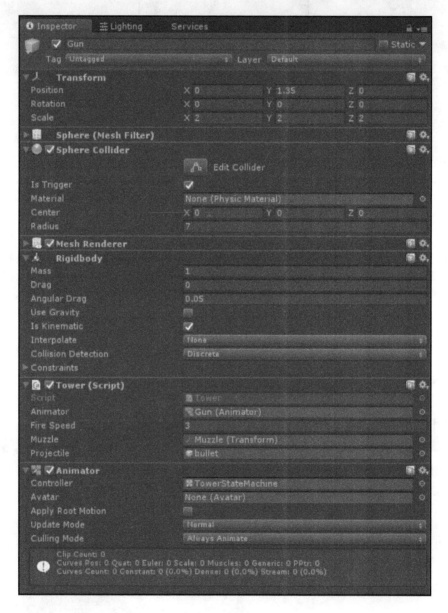

The inspector for the gun

There is quite a bit going on in the inspector here. Let's look at each of the components that affect the logic:

- **Sphere Collider**: This is essentially the tower's range. When the tank enters this sphere, the tower can detect it and will lock on to it to begin shooting at it. This is our implementation of perception for the tower. Notice that the radius is set to 7. The value can be changed to whatever you like, but 7 seems to be a fair value. Also, note that we set the **Is Trigger** checkbox to true. We don't want this sphere to actually cause collisions, just to fire trigger events.

- **Rigidbody**: This component is required for the collider to actually work properly, whether objects are moving or not. This is because Unity does not send collision or trigger events to game objects that are not moving, unless they have a `Rigidbody` component.

- **Tower**: This is the logic script for the tower. It works in tandem with the state machine and the state machine behavior, but we'll look at these components in more depth shortly.

- **Animator**: This is our tower's state machine. It doesn't actually handle animation.

Before we look at the code that drives the tower, let's take a brief look at the state machine. It's not terribly complicated, as you can see in the following screenshot:

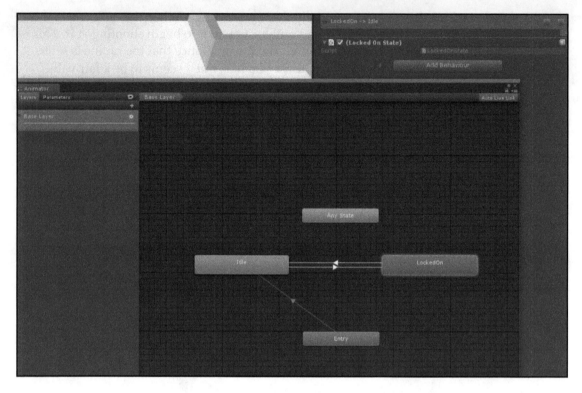

The state machine for the tower

There are two states that we care about: `Idle` (the default state) and `LockedOn`. The transition from `Idle` to `LockedOn` happens when the `TankInRange` bool is set to `true`, and the reverse transition happens when the bool is set to `false`.

The `LockedOn` state has a `StateMachineBehaviour` class attached to it, which we'll look at next:

```
using UnityEngine;
using System.Collections;

public class LockedOnState : StateMachineBehaviour {

    GameObject player;
    Tower tower;
```

```
    // OnStateEnter is called when a transition starts and the state machine
starts to evaluate this state
    override public void OnStateEnter(Animator animator, AnimatorStateInfo
stateInfo, int layerIndex) {
        player = GameObject.FindWithTag("Player");
        tower = animator.gameObject.GetComponent<Tower>();
        tower.LockedOn = true;
    }

    //OnStateUpdate is called on each Update frame between OnStateEnter
and OnStateExit callbacks
    override public void OnStateUpdate(Animator animator, AnimatorStateInfo
stateInfo, int layerIndex) {
        animator.gameObject.transform.LookAt(player.transform);
    }

    // OnStateExit is called when a transition ends and the state machine
finishes evaluating this state
    override public void OnStateExit(Animator animator, AnimatorStateInfo
stateInfo, int layerIndex) {
        animator.gameObject.transform.rotation = Quaternion.identity;
        tower.LockedOn = false;
    }
}
```

When we enter the state and `OnStateEnter` is called, we find a reference to our player. In the provided example, the player is tagged as `"Player"` so that we are able to get a reference to it using `GameObject.FindWithTag`. Next, we fetch a reference to the `Tower` component attached to our tower prefab and set its `LockedOn` bool to `true`.

As long as we're in the state, `OnStateUpdate` gets called on each frame. Inside this method, we get a reference to the `Gun GameObject` (which the `Tower` component is attached to) via the provided `Animator` reference. We use this reference to the gun to have it track the tank using `Transform.LookAt`.

 Alternatively, as the `LockedOn` bool of the `Tower` is set to `true`, this logic could be handled in the `Tower.cs` script instead.

Lastly, as we exit the state, `OnStateExit` gets called. We use this method to do a little cleanup. We reset the rotation of our gun to indicate that it is no longer tracking the player, and we set the tower's `LockedOn` bool back to `false`.

As we can see, this `StateMachineBehaviour` interacts with the `Tower.cs` script, so let's look at `Tower.cs` next for a bit more context as to what's happening:

```
using UnityEngine;
using System.Collections;

public class Tower : MonoBehaviour {
    [SerializeField]
    private Animator animator;

    [SerializeField]
    private float fireSpeed = 3f;
    private float fireCounter = 0f;
    private bool canFire = true;

    [SerializeField]
    private Transform muzzle;
    [SerializeField]
    private GameObject projectile;

    private bool isLockedOn = false;

    public bool LockedOn {
        get { return isLockedOn; }
        set { isLockedOn = value; }
    }
}
```

First up, we declare our variables and properties.

We need a reference to our state machine; this is where the `Animator` variable comes in. The next three variables, `fireSpeed`, `fireCounter`, and `canFire`, all relate to our tower's shooting logic. We'll see how that works later.

As we mentioned earlier, the muzzle is the location the bullets will spawn from when shooting. The projectile is the prefab we're going to instantiate.

Lastly, isLockedOn is get and set via LockedOn. While this book, in general, strays away from enforcing any particular coding convention, it's generally a good idea to keep values private unless explicitly required to be public, so instead of making isLockedOn public, we provide a property for it to access it remotely (in this case, from the LockedOnState behavior):

```
private void Update() {
        if (LockedOn && canFire) {
            StartCoroutine(Fire());
        }
    }

    private void OnTriggerEnter(Collider other) {
        if (other.tag == "Player") {
            animator.SetBool("TankInRange", true);
        }
    }

    private void OnTriggerExit(Collider other) {
        if (other.tag == "Player") {
            animator.SetBool("TankInRange", false);
        }
    }

    private void FireProjectile() {
        GameObject bullet = Instantiate(projectile, muzzle.position,
muzzle.rotation) as GameObject;
        bullet.GetComponent<Rigidbody>().AddForce(muzzle.forward * 300);
    }

    private IEnumerator Fire() {
        canFire = false;
        FireProjectile();
        while (fireCounter < fireSpeed) {
            fireCounter += Time.deltaTime;
            yield return null;
        }
        canFire = true;
        fireCounter = 0f;
    }
}
```

Next up, we have all our methods, and the meat and potatoes of the tower logic. Inside the `Update` loop, we check for two things—are we locked on, and can we fire? If both are true, we fire off our `Fire()` coroutine. We'll look at why `Fire()` is a coroutine before coming back to the `OnTrigger` messages.

> Coroutines can be a tricky concept to grasp if you're not already familiar with them. For more information on how to use them, check out Unity's documentation at `http://docs.unity3d.com/Manual/Coroutines.html`.

As we don't want our tower to be able to constantly shoot projectiles at the tank like a projectile-crazy death machine, we use the variables that we defined earlier to create a cushion between each shot. After we call `FireProjectile()` and set `canFire` to `false`, we start a counter from 0 up to `fireSpeed`, before we set `canFire` to `true` again. The `FireProjectile()` method handles the instantiation of the projectile and shoots it out toward the direction the gun is pointing to using `Rigidbody.AddForce`. The actual bullet logic is handled elsewhere, but we'll look at that later.

Lastly, we have our two `OnTrigger` events—one for when something enters the trigger attached to this component and another for when an object leaves said trigger. Remember the `TankInRange` bool that drives the transitions for our state machine? This variable gets set to `true` here when we enter the trigger and back to `false` as we exit. Essentially, when the tank enters the gun's sphere of "vision," it instantly locks on to the tank, and the lock is released when the tank leaves the sphere.

Making the towers shoot

If we look back at our `Tower` component in the inspector, you'll notice that a prefab named `bullet` is assigned to the `projectile` variable. This prefab can be found in the `Prefabs` folder of the sample project. The prefab looks similar to the following screenshot:

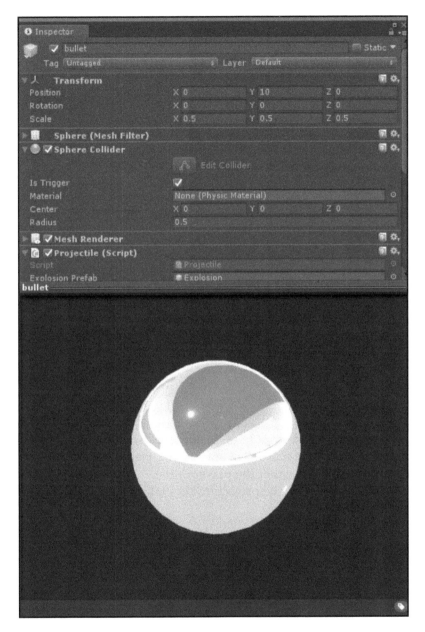

The bullet prefab

The `bullet` game object is nothing fancy; it's just a bright yellow orb. There is a sphere collider attached to it, and, once again, we must make sure that `IsTrigger` is set to `true` and it has a `Rigidbody` (with `gravity` turned `off`) attached to it. We also have a `Projectile` component attached to the `bullet` prefab. This handles the collision logic. Let's take a look at the code:

```
using UnityEngine;
using System.Collections;

public class Projectile : MonoBehaviour {

    [SerializeField]
    private GameObject explosionPrefab;

  void Start () {  }

    private void OnTriggerEnter(Collider other) {
        if (other.tag == "Player" || other.tag == "Environment") {
            if (explosionPrefab == null) {
                return;
            }
            GameObject explosion = Instantiate(explosionPrefab,
transform.position, Quaternion.identity) as GameObject;
            Destroy(this.gameObject);
        }
    }
}
```

We have a fairly straightforward script here. In our level, we have all of the floor and walls tagged as `"Environment"`, so in our `OnTriggerEnter` method, we check that the trigger this projectile is colliding with is either the player or the environment. If it is, we instantiate an `explosion` prefab and destroy the projectile. Let's take a look at the `explosion` prefab, which looks similar to this:

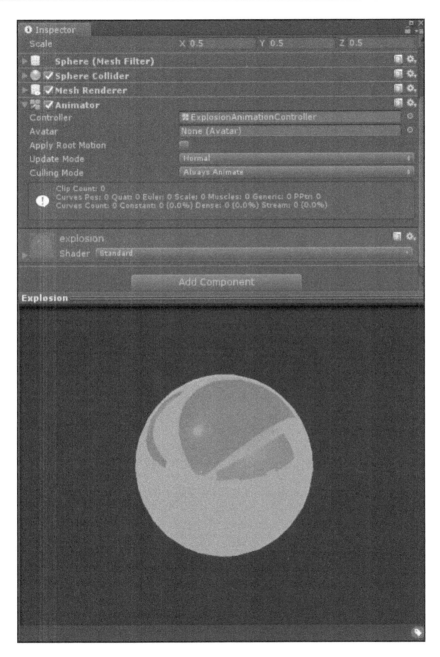

Inspector with the explosion prefab selected

As we can see, there is a very similar game object here; we have a sphere collider with `IsTrigger` set to `true`. The main difference is an `animator` component. When this `explosion` is instantiated, it expands as an explosion would, then we use the state machine to destroy the instance when it transitions out of its explosion state. The `animation` controller looks similar to the following screenshot:

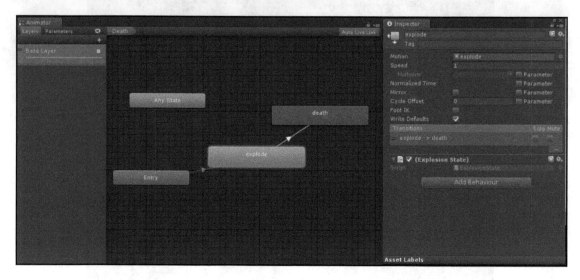

The animation controller driving the explosion prefab

You'll notice the `explode` state has a behavior attached to it. The code inside this behavior is fairly simple:

```
// OnStateExit is called when a transition ends and the state machine
finishes evaluating this state
    override public void OnStateExit(Animator animator, AnimatorStateInfo
stateInfo, int layerIndex) {
        Destroy(animator.gameObject, 0.1f);
    }
```

All we're doing here is destroying the instance of the object when we exit the state, which occurs when the animation ends.

If you want to flesh out the game with your own game logic, this may be a good place to trigger any secondary effects such as damage, environment particles, or anything you can think of!

Setting up the tank

The example project also includes a prefab for the tank, which is simply called (you guessed it) Tank, inside the Prefabs folder.

The tank itself is a simple agent with one goal: reach the end of the maze. As mentioned earlier, the player has to help the tank out along the way by activating its abilities to keep it safe from oncoming fire from the towers.

By now, you should be fairly familiar with the components you'll encounter along the way, except for the Tank.cs component attached to the prefab. Let's take a look at the code to figure out what's going on behind the scenes:

```
using UnityEngine;
using System.Collections;

public class Tank : MonoBehaviour {
    [SerializeField]
    private Transform goal;
    private NavMeshAgent agent;
    [SerializeField]
    private float speedBoostDuration = 3;
    [SerializeField]
    private ParticleSystem boostParticleSystem;
    [SerializeField]
    private float shieldDuration = 3f;
    [SerializeField]
    private GameObject shield;

    private float regularSpeed = 3.5f;
    private float boostedSpeed = 7.0f;
    private bool canBoost = true;
    private bool canShield = true;
```

There are a number of values that we want to be able to tweak easily, so we declare the corresponding variables first. Everything from the duration of our abilities to the effects associated with them is set here first:

```
    private bool hasShield = false;
    private void Start() {
        agent = GetComponent<NavMeshAgent>();
        agent.SetDestination(goal.position);
    }

    private void Update() {
        if (Input.GetKeyDown(KeyCode.B)) {
```

```
                   if (canBoost) {
                        StartCoroutine(Boost());
                   }
              }
              if (Input.GetKeyDown(KeyCode.S)) {
                   if (canShield) {
                        StartCoroutine(Shield());
                   }
              }
         }
    }
```

Our `Start` method simply does some setup for our tank; it grabs the `NavMeshAgent` component and sets its destination to be equal to our goal variable. We will discuss that in more detail soon.

We use the `Update` method to catch the input for our abilities. We've mapped `B` to `boost` and `S` to `shield`. As these are timed abilities, much like the towers' ability to shoot, we implement these via coroutines:

```
private IEnumerator Shield() {
     canShield = false;
     shield.SetActive(true);
     float shieldCounter = 0f;
     while (shieldCounter < shieldDuration) {
          shieldCounter += Time.deltaTime;
          yield return null;
     }
     canShield = true;
     shield.SetActive(false);
}

private IEnumerator Boost() {
     canBoost = false;
     agent.speed = boostedSpeed;
     boostParticleSystem.Play();
     float boostCounter = 0f;
     while (boostCounter < speedBoostDuration) {
          boostCounter += Time.deltaTime;
          yield return null;
     }
     canBoost = true;
     boostParticleSystem.Pause();
     agent.speed = regularSpeed;
}
```

The two abilities' logic is very similar. The `shield` enables and disables the `shield` game object, which we define in a variable in the inspector, and after an amount of time equal to `shieldDuration` has passed, we turn it off and allow the player to use the `shield` again.

The main difference in the `Boost` code is that rather than enabling and disabling a game object, the `boost` calls `Play` on a particle system we assign via the inspector and also sets the speed of our `NavMeshAgent` to double the original value, before resetting it at the end of the ability's duration.

 Can you think of other abilities you'd give the tank? This is a very straightforward pattern that you can use to implement new abilities in your own variant of the project. You can also add additional logic to customize the shield and boost abilities here.

The sample scene already has an instance of the tank in it with all the variables properly set up. The inspector for the tank in the sample scene looks similar to the following screenshot:

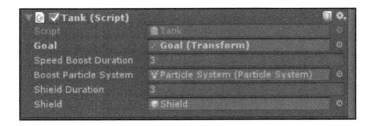

Inspector with the tank instance selected

As you can see in the preceding screenshot, we've assigned the `Goal` variable to a transform with the same name, which is located in the scene at the end of the maze we've set up. We can also tweak the duration of our abilities here, which is set to **3** by default. You can also swap out the art for the abilities, be it the particle system used in the boost or the game object used for the shield.

The last bit of code to look at is the code driving the camera. We want the camera to follow the player, but only along its z value, horizontally down the track. The code to achieve this looks similar to this:

```
using UnityEngine;
using System.Collections;

public class HorizontalCam : MonoBehaviour {
    [SerializeField]
    private Transform target;
```

```
        private Vector3 targetPositon;

        private void Update() {
            targetPositon = transform.position;
            targetPositon.z = target.transform.position.z;
            transform.position = Vector3.Lerp(transform.position,
    targetPositon, Time.deltaTime);
        }
    }
```

As you can see, we simply set the target position of the camera equal to its current position on all axes, but we then assign the z axis of the target position to be the same as our target's, which, if you look in the inspector, has been set to the transform of the tank. We then use linear interpolation (`Vector3.Lerp`) to smoothly translate the camera from its current position to its target position every frame.

Bonus tank abilities

The sample project also includes three bonus tank abilities for you to play with. Of course, you are highly encouraged to modify these abilities or implement your own custom rules, but for the sake of spicing up the example a bit, all you have to do is add the component for each ability you want to add to the tank prefab.

The bonus abilities are:

- **Hulk mode**: Your tank grows in size for a set amount of time. Want a challenge? Implement a health and armor system similar to our *HomeRock* example from `Chapter 6`, *Behavior Trees*, and have the buff be represented visually by this ability!
- **Shrink mode**: It's the opposite of hulk mode, duh! Your tank shrinks for a set period of time. If you're feeling up to the task, try implementing a stealth system where turrets are unable to detect your tank while it's in shrink mode.
- **Time warp, or as I like to call it, DMV mode**: This ability slooooows down time to a crawl. If you want a real challenge, try implementing a selective weapon system, where the turrets could try to outsmart you by using a faster projectile to counter your time warp mode!

Where you take the abilities system is up to you. It's always fun to see what different directions readers take their own versions of these samples. If you have a cool twist on this or any of the previous samples, share them with the author via Twitter (@ray_barrera).

Setting up the environment

As our tank uses a `NavMeshAgent` component to traverse the environment, we need to set up our scene using static game objects for the bake process to work properly, as we learned in `Chapter 4`, *Finding Your Way*. The maze is set up in a way so that towers are spread out fairly reasonably and the tank has plenty of space to maneuver around easily. The following screenshot shows the general layout of the maze:

The gauntlet our tank must run through

As you can see, there are seven towers spread out through the maze and a few twists and turns for our tank to break line of sight. In order to avoid having our tank graze the walls, we adjust the settings in the navigation window to our liking. By default, the example scene has the agent radius set to 1.46 and the step height to 1.6. There are no hard rules for how we arrived at these numbers; it is just trial and error.

After baking the NavMesh, we'll end up with something similar to what's shown in the following screenshot:

The scene after we've baked our NavMesh

Feel free to rearrange the walls and towers to your liking. Just remember that any blocking objects you add to the scene must be marked as static, and you have to rebake the navigation for the scene after you've set everything up just the way you like it.

Testing the example

The example scene is ready to play right out of the box, so if you didn't get the itch to modify any of the default settings, you can just hit the play button and watch your tank go. You'll notice we've added a canvas with a label explaining the controls to the player. There is nothing fancy going on here; it's just a simple "press this button to do that" kind of instruction:

Simple instructions to guide the player

The example project is a great example to expand upon and to have fun with. With the concepts learned throughout this book, you can expand on the types of towers, the tank's abilities, the rules, or even give the tank more complex, nuanced behavior. For now, we can see that the concepts of state machines, navigation, perception and sensing, and steering, all come together in a simple yet amusing example. The following screenshot shows the game in action:

The tank-defense game in action

Summary

So, we've reached the end. In this chapter, we took a few of the concepts covered in the book and applied them to create a small tank-defense game. We built upon the concept of finite state machines, which we originally covered in `Chapter 2`, *Finite State Machines and You*, and created an artificial intelligence to drive our enemy towers' behavior. We then enhanced the behavior by combining it with sensing and perception, and finally we implemented navigation via Unity's NavMesh feature to help our tank AI navigate through our maze-like level, through a gauntlet of autonomous AI towers with one thing on their simple AI minds: destroy!

As we conclude this book, take a moment and pat yourself on the back! We've covered a lot of ground, and covered a lot of topics. You've now learned about state machines, behavior trees, A*, fuzzy logic, and so much more. What's most exciting is to think of all the ways in which you can mix-and-match and apply these concepts. Hopefully, throughout this book you've been thinking of ways to enhance your existing or upcoming games with these concepts. You now have the tools to create smarter inhabitants for your digital worlds. Good luck!

Other Books You May Enjoy

If you enjoyed this book, you may be interested in these other books by Packt:

Practical Game AI Programming
Micael DaGraca

ISBN: 978-1-78712-281-9

- Get to know the basics of how to create different AI for different type of games
- Know what to do when something interferes with the AI choices and how the AI should behave if that happens
- Plan the interaction between the AI character and the environment using Smart Zones or Triggering Events
- Use animations correctly, blending one animation into another and rather than stopping one animation and starting another
- Calculate the best options for the AI to move using Pruning Strategies, Wall Distances, Map Preprocess Implementation, and Forced Neighbours
- Create Theta algorithms to the AI to find short and realistic looking paths
- Add many characters into the same scene and make them behave like a realistic crowd

Mastering Unity 2017 Game Development with C# - Second Edition
Alan Thorn

ISBN: 978-1-78847-983-7

- Explore hands-on tasks and real-world scenarios to make a Unity horror adventure game
- Create enemy characters that act intelligently and make reasoned decisions
- Use data files to save and restore game data in a way that is platform-agnostic
- Get started with VR development
- Use navigation meshes, occlusion culling, and Profiler tools
- Work confidently with GameObjects, rotations, and transformations
- Understand specific gameplay features such as AI enemies, inventory systems, and level design

Unity 2017 Game Optimization - Second Edition
Chris Dickinson

ISBN:9781-7-8839-236-5

- Use the Unity Profiler to find bottlenecks anywhere in your application, and discover how to resolve them
- Implement best practices for C# scripting to avoid common pitfalls
- Develop a solid understanding of the rendering pipeline, and maximize its performance by reducing draw calls and avoiding fill rate bottlenecks
- Enhance shaders in a way that is accessible to most developers, optimizing them through subtle yet effective performance tweaks
- Keep your scenes as dynamic as possible by making the most of the Physics engine
- Organize, filter, and compress your art assets to maximize performance while maintaining high quality
- Discover different kinds of performance problems that are critical for VR projects and how to tackle them
- Use the Mono Framework and C# to implement low-level enhancements that maximize memory usage and avoid garbage collection
- Get to know the best practices for project organization to save time through an improved workflow

Leave a review - let other readers know what you think

Please share your thoughts on this book with others by leaving a review on the site that you bought it from. If you purchased the book from Amazon, please leave us an honest review on this book's Amazon page. This is vital so that other potential readers can see and use your unbiased opinion to make purchasing decisions, we can understand what our customers think about our products, and our authors can see your feedback on the title that they have worked with Packt to create. It will only take a few minutes of your time, but is valuable to other potential customers, our authors, and Packt. Thank you!

Index

www.ingramcontent.com/pod-product-compliance
Lightning Source LLC
Chambersburg PA
CBHW080636060326
40690CB00021B/4956